THE STRUGGLE IS OVER!

You Have the Mind of Christ!

By Connie Witter

The Struggle is Over! You Have The Mind of Christ!
ISBN: 978-0-578-56591-0
Copyright © 2019 Because of Jesus Publishing
P.O. Box 3064
Broken Arrow, OK 74013-3064

Cover Design by: Nancy Bishop
nbishopsdesigns.com

Editing and Interior Design by: Yattira Editing Services
contact@yattira.com

Printed in the United States of America.

Contents

Endorsements

I recently had the privilege of pre-reading my friend, Connie Witter's book. I have a personal rule that I won't give a written endorsement for any book before reading every word of it. After reading this book, I am so excited and honored to endorse it!

I couldn't be happier that the Holy Spirit downloaded this revelation of the mind of Christ in Connie's heart so she could then upload it to the Church!

Wow! Just, wow! I believe the revelation within these pages is critically needed among Christians today. Connie's book is extremely encouraging. It clearly proves that it is 100% possible for Believers across this planet to live free from struggle, if they will only embrace their true identity about the brand-new mind they have been given as part of their new creation identity in Christ!

Sandra McCollom
Author of *I Tried Until I Almost Died*

I have to say, this book has changed my life! The revelation that the struggle is over, and I have the mind of Christ, has had so much effect in my thoughts and heart, and I have seen the results!

This revelation has caused my daughter, who was gone from me for 18 years, to return to her first love, Jesus! Not only is she completely off of drugs, she is reminding us daily that she has the mind of Christ! She and her newly married husband are so full of this revelation that I see their lives being transformed by leaps and bounds!

I had heard, and read, that we have the mind of Christ for over 40 years, but I never knew that it truly was the only mind that I have! I don't have another mind. Negative thoughts are not mine! The only thoughts I own are the thoughts and purposes of Jesus' heart!

This has transformed me, my marriage, my daughter, my husband, and our whole family! My husband and I pastor a church in Redlands, California and everyone at our church has been hearing this truth. Now they are saying that they have the mind of Christ also!

As the saying goes, "The proof is in the pudding!" Well, that certainly fits here! Having heard Connie teach these messages, and now reading this book, has proven results at True Grace Church! When Connie preached this message at our church, many people in our congregation began listening to her Bible study series on the mind of Christ on YouTube, and now we all declare over ourselves and each other, "We have the mind of Christ!"

I thank the Lord for this revelation of His love and good-ness toward us! Thank you, Connie for writing this book and for showing us the truth about our identity in Christ! I am so excited to teach this book at our church as well!

Heather Holley Baeumel
Co-pastor of True Grace Church
Redlands, CA

Real People! Real Freedom!
What Others Are Saying About This Teaching

This is such a great message! I need to hear it over and over to realize that negative thoughts are not my thoughts because I have the mind of Christ. The mind of Christ is part of my righteousness/identity package. It's so, so powerful!

- Marsha

This is revelation of such an incredible nature! Connie, you are sending out powerful missiles with every line of God's heart and Word revealed! Missiles that destroy the strongholds of the enemy and every speculation that sets itself up against the true knowledge of God! This is big, and I don't think we even realize how big! This is powerful; we can receive the mind of Christ and walk free of the torment of the flesh and our own perceived failures! Please keep up the marvelous work of grace!

– Lauree

This truth is life-changing! Negative thoughts are not my thoughts! I believe the best because the mind of Christ is the mind of love!

– Amy

I think God's thoughts towards others! I have the mind of Christ! Thank you, Connie! This is a life-changing message. Awesome!

– Gwen

Let God change the way we think! It's all about our identity! If we get that down inside of us, what a transformed life! We would reign in life—our trying days are over!

– Cindy

I'm in my bed right now, and this is putting me on fire! Wow, a revelation: the mind of Christ is grace!

– Rebecca

THERE'S NOTHING WRONG WITH MY MIND! I HAVE THE MIND OF CHRIST! The mind of Christ believes the best! Wow! This is powerful.

– Chell

Just sitting over here crying; don't mind me. I'm so thankful you shared with me what it means to have the mind of Christ! It's life-changing, and I will never go back to thinking on my own. "Your thoughts run your life"—that's about as powerful a statement as I've ever heard. Negative thoughts are not in my salvation package. Don't stop teaching!

– Jessica

Such FREEDOM in knowing my identity in CHRIST and that I HAVE THE MIND OF CHRIST!

– Louise

I have struggled all my life, trying to make this Christian life work, trying to transform my mind. It's been so hard. But now I hear: Let God do it.

– Cindy

This revelation of the mind of Christ is changing me on the inside. I was thinking so wrong, and still doing a lot in my own strength, without even realizing it. I have understood grace for a long time now, but this mind-of-Christ revelation is changing everything. It is helping me to love and pray for people, even when they are not nice. Before, I would just get offended and write them off. But no more! The beauty of this is that the Holy Spirit is empowering me to walk in my true identity.

– Susan

I have been to hell and back, but suddenly, I'm experiencing the Holy Spirit doing a healing in my mind and attitude toward myself and healing things that I had buried from my past. Bless you!

– Beatrice

I've been a Christian most of my life, yet I was defeated and condemned daily. I was always saying, "God, there has to be more; I'm a miserable Christian. Is it me?" I felt like a failure in everything. I began listening to your mind-of-Christ teaching on YouTube and God began to change the way I think: how I see myself and how I see Him. I'm even seeing the storms I'm going through differently now. The Holy Spirit has given me the answer but walking through has been difficult. When I begin to struggle and get in fear, I sweetly hear Jesus say, "You're taking your eyes off Me." I say, "Okay, Lord, I have Your mind about this and I look to You." I just wanted to share and say thank you, for I am a life that is changing because of your teachings and sharing what God did for you.

– Sandy

Earlier this year, you came to True Grace in Redlands, California. I purchased your CD "I Have the Mind of Christ". I had never heard you speak before but felt led by the Spirit to buy that CD. Well, let me just tell you, every single day I have been listening to it over and over and over again. It has changed my heart and my mind. I saw the fruit of this in April of this year when I dropped off my sweet Sarah (she's 10) at a birthday party. She was in a jumper, playing with her little friend, when a girl fell on her thumb. I got that dreaded call from the mom, "Your daughter got hurt and she needs to go to the ER." Instantly I heard, "I have the mind of Christ."

My natural reaction is to get anxious when I hear stuff like this concerning my kids. But on that day, I knew that I would not be letting the lies of the enemy overtake me with all the "what ifs". When I picked her up, the mom—a nurse—began to tell me gloomy details of what she thought. I kindly took my girl and came against that report because I have the mind of Christ and I refuse to believe the lies of the enemy. To make a long story short, Sarah's thumb wasn't broken. She only had a small fracture, and she didn't need to have it painfully set. For me, this was a huge victory! I want you to know that my beautiful 10-year-old girl has listened to this CD so many times with me and now confesses, "I have the mind of Christ." You have no idea what that does for this Mama! I homeschool her, and for her elective class this year, we will be studying your new book, *The Struggle Is Over! You Have the Mind of Christ!* Thank you for spending time with Jesus; I have been enjoying the fruit of that in your books, CD, and YouTube channel. Connie, thank you for sharing the truth of what the Word of God really says.

– Mariam

This teaching is powerful and gives rest to the mind. Finally, the struggle is really over! Thank you, Connie Witter, for explaining the truth.

– Flower

Personal Note from the Author

What I am about to share with you in this book has been absolutely mind-changing and mind-blowing for me! To understand the mind of Christ as our true identity, and embrace it in every situation of our lives, literally has the power to bring forth God's kingdom on the earth, and to bring His plan and purpose to pass in your life!

Have you ever struggled with fearful or negative thoughts about yourself, others, or a difficult situation you were facing? Proverbs 4:23 tells us, *"Be careful what you think, because your thoughts shape your life."*

Negative thoughts are toxic. Scientists have proven 87-95% of physical and mental illness comes from negative thoughts! Negative thoughts destroy your health, your relationships, and your dreams! That's how imperative it is to know and embrace the truth about your mind. It's a matter of life or death.

What we think becomes what we believe and, ultimately, what we experience in our lives. That's how important it is to renew your mind with the truth. But whose job is it to renew your mind? You might be surprised to find out! What does it mean to have the mind of Christ? Did you know that negative thoughts are not your thoughts? You'll learn the answer to these questions, and so much more, as you read through each chapter.

Jesus said in John 8:32, *"If you embrace the truth it will release more freedom into your life!"* (TPT).

What if you believed the truth about your mind? How would that change your everyday life? Imagine a mind free from depression, free from fear, free from stress, free from guilt and shame, free from the fear of what others think, and free from every negative thought that limits your potential. Jesus said, "All things are possible to those who believe!" (Mark 9:23).

When you believe you have the mind of Christ, something amazing begins to happen! I have received testimonies from around the world from people who have experienced freedom from addictions, depression, fear, anxiety, and condemnation as the Holy Spirit has made this truth come alive in their hearts. I have shared some of these testimonies in this book.

It is my prayer that the same thing will happen in your mind and in your life as you receive this powerful truth that the mind of Christ is your true identity in Jesus! It truly does have the power to end the struggle in your mind and bring you into a place of perfect peace and rest in Jesus. I pray that you will experience the power outflowing from His resurrection! *The Struggle is Over! You Have the Mind of Christ!* You are one with Him! (John 17:20-23).

Connie Witter

Founder of Because of Jesus Ministries
(www.becauseofjesus.com)

Founder of Women of Grace Conferences
(www.womenofgrace.us)

If you would like to listen to the teachings that go along with this book or are interested in leading a group through this Bible study, you can watch them on my YouTube ministry channel at www.youtube.com/conniewitter.

Chapter 1

The Mind of Christ is Your True Identity!

The true Gospel of Jesus Christ is all about identity. When we understand who we truly are in Jesus, and embrace it, we reign as kings in life through Him.

Romans 5:17 says, *"...much more surely will those who receive [God's] overflowing grace (unmerited favor) and the free gift of righteousness [putting them into right standing with Himself] reign as kings in life through the one Man Jesus Christ (the Messiah, the Anointed One)"* (AMPC).

For the first twenty years of my Christian life, I did not reign in life through Jesus! I did not experience the peace and joy that Jesus promised me. The reason for this was because I was not receiving God's grace and His free gift of righteousness as my true identity. As a result, I was constantly struggling to be good enough and qualify myself for God's blessing. I spent all those years in self-effort, trying to be pleasing to God and be who He wanted me to be.

Finally, I came to the end of my self-effort, and I cried out to Jesus to show me the truth that would set me free. That day, the Holy Spirit led me to the truth and revealed to me

1

my true identity in Jesus. I finally understood that I am the righteousness of God in Christ Jesus as a gift of His grace.

My struggle to be good enough ended that day when I embraced the truth that I am accepted, approved, blessed, qualified and perfectly righteous—not because of anything that I have done, but because of what Jesus has done for me. He has made me one with Him and given me His righteous identity.

I remember the Holy Spirit revealing to me that my trying days were over. I recall hearing these words in my heart, "Connie, you don't have to try anymore. Just embrace what I say about you. Believe what I see when I look at you, and I will bring forth the fruit in your life!" That began my journey out of a life of self-effort and into the amazing grace of my Savior, Jesus! He had given me a brand-new identity and all I had to do was embrace it! That day, I embraced the truth that I am the righteousness of God in Christ Jesus, and I began to reign in life through Him!

I have been growing in grace and my identity in Christ for a long time, but on one particular day, I found myself struggling again. I was struggling with fear and worry about a situation concerning one of my daughters. I started having the "what-ifs?" come up in my mind. I thought, "What if this happens, or what if that happens?" It was a sense of fearful foreboding that I could not shake.

I knew the promises of God. I knew that I am the righteousness of God in Christ Jesus, and I began to speak what God said is true, but for some reason, the negative thoughts came back even stronger. I couldn't get rid of the fearful thoughts that were bombarding my mind. The struggle was real, and I felt like I was drowning underneath these oppressive thoughts. For three days, I really struggled with these negative thoughts.

Now, that's not how I normally live. Jesus has brought me to a place where my heart is normally at peace, so this experience was foreign to me. I usually feel very confident and secure in what my good Father says about me, so I didn't understand what was happening.

On the 3rd day, I said, "Father, what is happening to me? Why can't I get victory over these negative thoughts? Show me the truth that will set me free!"

Just like He always does, He spoke to my heart and revealed to me something about my identity that set me free.

One hundred percent of the time, when we are struggling with negative thoughts, it's a case of mistaken identity. We're believing something about who God is, or who we are, that is not true.

Whenever I feel myself struggling, I know I need a fresh revelation of who I am in Christ. That is the only place I have ever found true, lasting peace and joy. So that day, as I listened to the Holy Spirit within me, I heard, "Connie, you have the mind of Christ. Embrace your true identity concerning your thoughts and your mind."

Immediately, 1 Corinthians 2:16 (which tells us that we have the mind of Christ) came into my thoughts. I had never really thought of the mind of Christ as part of my identity. I had quoted that Scripture, and believed it, but the Holy Spirit was giving me a much deeper revelation. It was a revelation about my identity concerning my mind and my thoughts that would change my life forever!

Let's read the full context of 1 Corinthians 2:9-16:

"This is why the Scriptures say: Things never discovered or heard of before, things beyond our ability to imagine—these are the many things God has in store for all his lovers.

3

10 But God now unveils these profound realities to us by the Spirit. Yes, he has revealed to us his inmost heart and deepest mysteries through the Holy Spirit, who constantly explores all things. 11 After all, who can really see into a person's heart and know his hidden impulses except for that person's spirit? So it is with God. His thoughts and secrets are only fully understood by his Spirit, the Spirit of God.

12 For we did not receive the spirit of this world system but the Spirit of God, so that we might come to understand and experience all that grace has lavished upon us. 13 And we articulate these realities with the words imparted to us by the Spirit and not with the words taught by human wisdom. We join together Spirit-revealed truths with Spirit-revealed words. 14 Someone living on an entirely human level rejects the revelations of God's Spirit, for they make no sense to him. He can't understand the revelations of the Spirit because they are only discovered by the illumination of the Spirit. 15 Those who live in the Spirit are able to carefully evaluate all things, and they are subject to the scrutiny of no one but God" (TPT).

16 For who has known or understood the mind (the counsels and purposes) of the Lord so as to guide and instruct Him and give Him knowledge? But we have the mind of Christ (the Messiah) and do hold the thoughts (feelings and purposes) of His heart" (AMPC).

As I thought upon verse 16, the word "have" jumped out at me. The mind of Christ was not something I was trying to get. This Scripture said I "have" it! This word "have" means "to make it your own; to possess; to lay hold of" (blueletterbible.com).

This means that I own the mind of Christ! I possess the mind of Christ! I lay hold of His thoughts, feelings and the purposes of His heart as my true identity. WOW! A light bulb came on that day. The Holy Spirit revealed to me that Jesus had already won this struggle I was having in my thoughts by giving me His very mind.

I had never really thought of it like that before. I believed that Scripture. I had quoted that verse at times, but I had never really embraced it as part of my righteous identity in Christ. I had not applied it every day to each negative thought that tried to enter my mind.

However, as I laid hold of this truth about my true identity with both hands, my life was about to dramatically change! The devil had lost and I had won because I have the mind of Christ! That day I owned it! That was what was true about my mind, and that day, the negative thoughts lost their power in my life. They were not my thoughts, so they could not define my life.

I simply said, "Father, fill my mind with Your thoughts, feelings, and purposes concerning this situation in my daughter's life. I have the mind of Christ about this!" Then the most amazing thing happened! I heard the Father speak deep within my heart, "Connie, not only do you have the mind of Christ, but your daughter does too!"

I began to cry happy tears as I realized that everything I ever wanted for my daughter—that her mind would be filled with the thoughts, feelings, and purposes of God's heart for her life—was true about her! The Holy Spirit had manifested the mind of Christ in my thoughts. I could now see from His perspective.

The peace of God began to flood my soul as supernatural faith rose up to believe what my good Father said about me and my daughter. From that day forward, it didn't matter what I saw in the natural. What my Father said about her was true! Just like Romans 5:17 says, as I received God's grace, and embraced the truth that both she and I have the mind of Christ, the struggle was over, and I began to reign over all those negative thoughts.

We experience the Mind of Christ by the Power of God's Spirit

Now let's take a closer look at 1 Corinthians 2:9-16. Notice how many times this passage of Scripture says that we experience the mind of Christ, "by the Spirit," "of the Spirit," "through the Spirit," and "in the Spirit." In these verses, we see so clearly that when we embrace the truth that we have the mind of Christ, the Spirit of God brings forth that fruit in us.

For example, when I first embraced the truth that I am the righteousness of God in Christ Jesus, my struggle to be good enough was over, and the Spirit of God began to bring forth the fruit of righteousness in my life. The same thing happened when I embraced the mind of Christ as my true identity. The struggle with those fearful, negative thoughts was over, and the Spirit of God began to illuminate my mind with the very thoughts, feelings and purposes of God's heart concerning my situation.

Verses 9-10 tell us that the thoughts of God are beyond our ability to imagine, but that they are revealed to us by the Spirit. We often depend on our own ability to understand something or think correctly. We may even think, "I just need to get this!" But these verses make it very clear to us that it is not by our own ability that we experience the mind of Christ. Revelation and understanding come to us by the Holy Spirit within us. Our good Father has revealed to us His inmost heart and thoughts through the power of the Holy Spirit. In Christ, we possess His heart and His thoughts!

1 Corinthians 2:12 says, *"For we did not receive the spirit of this world system but the Spirit of God, so that we*

might come to understand and experience all that grace has lavished upon us" (TPT).

The world's system is filled with man's thoughts, feelings, opinions and judgments about everything. The world's way of thinking leads to depression, pride, division, judgementalism, fear, guilt, and condemnation. But the Spirit of God reveals God's thoughts, feelings, and opinions about everything! His mind and thoughts are filled with love, joy, peace, patience, kindness, goodness, faith, humility, and self-control (Galatians 5:22-23).

We have been given the Holy Spirit so that we might come to understand and experience all that grace has lavished upon us. We possess as our new identity His very mind! We have the mind of Christ. We are not trying to think right. We think right by the power of His Spirit. 2 Timothy 1:7 says, *"For God has not given us a spirit of fear, but of power and of love and of a sound mind"* (NKJV).

1 Corinthians 2:14-15 says, *"Someone living on an entirely human level rejects the revelations of God's Spirit, for they make no sense to him. He can't understand the revelations of the Spirit because they are only discovered by the illumination of the Spirit. Those who live in the Spirit are able to carefully evaluate all things, and they are subject to the scrutiny of no one but God"* (TPT).

Someone living entirely on a human level rejects the revelation of the mind of Christ because it makes no sense to them. They believe it's entirely up to them to change the way they think. They struggle to change the way they think instead of depending on Jesus within them.

One reason a believer does not experience the mind of Christ is because they are still trying in their own ability. But those who depend on the Spirit within them experience the mind of Christ by the illumination of the Spirit. Those who live in the Spirit (embrace their true identity and rely on His power within them) evaluate all things, but they are not subject to what any other human thinks of them. They find their identity in the thoughts, feelings, and purposes of God's heart toward them in Christ.

We've heard many messages on the importance of renewing our minds. Those messages often point to our self-effort to renew our minds. Do our minds need to be renewed? Yes, they do, but it comes by the Spirit. Religion and the world's system focuses on man's ability and human effort, but the kingdom of God is all about the Spirit's ability within us.

We did not receive the spirit of this world's system that tells us to try harder. We received the Spirit of God who reminds us that we have the mind of Christ and then manifests that truth in our lives.

Every Struggle Begins in the Mind

The word struggle means "to make strenuous efforts in the face of difficulties or opposition; struggling with a problem; to proceed with difficulty or with great effort" (dictionary.com).

Every emotional struggle begins in our minds. The way we think and believe determines our failure or success in every area of our lives. Trying to believe right and do right by our own self-effort causes us to struggle. Jesus came to deliver us from our self-effort. He said, "Are you tired and worn out? Come to me, and I will give you rest. I will teach you how to live freely and lightly" (Matthew 11:28-30).

That day when I came to Jesus, He taught me how to live freely and lightly by reminding me of who I am in Him. When I let go of my self-effort and owned the mind of Christ as my true identity, the struggle with those negative thoughts was over! Embracing identity is a very powerful, spiritual thing that changes everything in a person's life.

The world says, "The struggle is real! You need to try harder to overcome this battle in your mind. You need to exert strenuous effort to think right and do right so you can have a good life." That's self-effort!

Jesus says, "The struggle is over! I overcame this battle for you! I gave you My mind! You can let go of your strenuous self-effort and let Me bring forth the fruit in your life." That's grace!

What you think about yourself determines the very course of your life. Proverbs 4:23 says, *"Be careful how you think; your life is shaped by your thoughts"* (GNT).

What you think about yourself, what you think about others, and what you think about a situation you are facing will determine the condition of your heart and what you will experience in your life. Your whole life is shaped by your thoughts! That's how imperative it is that you embrace the truth that you have the mind of Christ. By doing so, you can experience the abundant life that your good Father has planned for you. Proverbs 23:7 says that as a man thinks within himself, so is he. The Scriptures are very clear that what a man thinks of himself is what he experiences in his life.

The Good News is, you don't have to be controlled by negative thoughts anymore. You can let the Holy Spirit change the way you think by embracing your true identity in Jesus. You hold the thoughts, feelings, and purposes of God's heart. As Jesus is, so are you in this world (1 John 4:17). So, the next time you find yourself struggling with a negative thought, you can boldly say, "I have the mind of Christ! I trust You, Holy Spirit, to manifest that truth in my thoughts right now." The Holy Spirit will illuminate your mind with the thoughts, feelings and purposes of God's heart.

When this powerful, life-changing truth first came to my mind, I shared it with my daughter-in-law, Jessica Witter. I shared with her how the Holy Spirit revealed to me that the mind of Christ was our true identity. His mind is filled with love, joy, and peace. I explained that when we don't understand and embrace this truth, we struggle with negative thoughts about ourselves and others our entire lives. But when we come to the throne of grace and receive the truth that we have the mind of Christ, the struggle is over, and the Spirit of God illuminates our minds with the truth that sets us free.

I could tell she was very interested in what I was sharing because all of us have struggled with negative thoughts at times. The next day, I talked with her on the phone and she said, "I couldn't sleep last night because I was thinking about what you shared about us having the mind of Christ. I was lying in bed, struggling with negative thoughts about my purpose. I was wondering, *Am I doing enough? Should I be doing more?* Then I turned my thoughts to Jesus and said, 'Father, I thank You that I have the mind of Christ!' Then the Holy Spirit began to reveal truth to me that brought peace to my heart."

Jessica began to share with me this wonderful truth that the Holy Spirit revealed to her about the mind of Christ in the moment of Jesus' greatest struggle. He was in the garden of Gethsemane getting ready to lay His life down for the world. The Bible says He was struck with terror. He was struggling with doubts and fears concerning fulfilling His purpose to the point of sweating great drops of blood. Can you imagine what anxiety and stress He must have been struggling with in that moment? Jesus, the Savior of the world, has compassion on you when you struggle because He knows what it feels like to struggle in your mind with negative thoughts. The struggle was real! But something powerful was about to happen!

Jesus came to the Father—the throne of grace—to receive strength in His time of need. In that moment, Jesus revealed the mind of Christ when He laid down His human fears, and ways of thinking, and embraced the Father's thoughts, feelings and purpose for His life. Jesus prayed this powerful prayer, "Father, not My will, but Yours be done!"

Something amazing happened when Jesus owned the Father's mind and thoughts as His own. Shortly after that prayer, Jesus came out of the Garden of Gethsemane empowered by the Spirit and at perfect peace, ready to lay His life down for the sins of the entire world and fulfill His purpose on this earth! The struggle was over! Jesus reigned over every fear because the Holy Spirit manifested the thoughts and purpose of the Father's heart in His mind.

What a powerful example of coming to the throne of grace for help and embracing the mind of the Father in those moments when we struggle with our own doubts and fears. What is the mind of Christ in those moments? "Father, not my will, but Yours be done!"

In other words, "Father, I ask for Your strength right now. I embrace Your mind about this situation. I trust You to manifest Your thoughts, feelings, and purposes in my mind right now."

That's exactly what Jessica did in that moment when she was struggling with thoughts concerning her purpose. She asked for help and embraced that she had the mind of Christ, and the Holy Spirit brought peace to her thoughts and her mind. What a powerful revelation the Holy Spirit brought to Jessica's mind that day, and it blessed me so much!

Before this conversation with my daughter-in-law, I remember asking the Lord, "Is it really this easy? We just embrace that we have the mind of Christ, and the Holy Spirit manifests that truth in our lives? Show me this in someone else because it is working so beautifully for me." Jesus used

11

Jessica to show me that it really is that simple. It's amazing how the struggle in our soul really does end when we come to the throne of grace and receive what our good Father says about us (Hebrews 4:16). James 4:6 says that God gives His grace to those who are humble enough to receive it. When we believe our good Father, the struggle ends, and we enter into rest! (Hebrews 4:3).

God's Thoughts Are Your Thoughts and His Ways Are Your Ways!

One of the scriptures that has brought confusion about our identity concerning our minds is found in Isaiah 55:7-9. In this passage of Scripture, God says, "My thoughts are not your thoughts!" For many years, I quoted that scripture and embraced it as what was true about me. I heard it in church. It sounded right, so I embraced it, but it was a lie. The enemy often takes scriptures out of context to deceive God's children into believing something that is not true.

Let's read Isaiah 55:7-9 in context:

"7 Let the wicked forsake his way and the unrighteous man his thoughts; and let him return to the Lord, and He will have love, pity, and mercy for him, and to our God, for He will multiply to him His abundant pardon.

8 For My thoughts are not your thoughts, neither are your ways My ways, says the Lord.

9 For as the heavens are higher than the earth, so are My ways higher than your ways and My thoughts than your thoughts" (AMPC).

Many of us have quoted this verse as the truth about ourselves all our lives, yet God is not even talking to believers in these verses. He is talking to the wicked and unrighteous. Have you accepted Jesus as your Savior? Are you righteous in Christ (Romans 3:21-26)? If the answer is, "Yes!" then why have we accepted this as the truth about us?

In these verses, God is talking to the unrighteous man, and you're not unrighteous. So, don't believe that lie anymore. Embrace the truth that you have the mind of Christ. You are righteous in Jesus, and your thoughts are His thoughts. His ways are your ways. You are one with Him (John 17:20-23)! You have His mind and you hold the thoughts, feelings, and purposes of His heart.

So many thoughts go through our minds each day. Imagine for a moment what your life would look like if you embraced the mind of Christ as your true identity whenever a negative thought entered your mind. The Spirit of God would illuminate your mind with Christ's perspective. Just like Jesus, you'd experience His perfect peace in every situation. You would say only what you hear your Father say, and you'd experience the manifestation of His glory in your life. You would truly begin to experience the fullness of life that Jesus came to give you!

So, let's embrace our true identity in Christ together:

Father, I thank You that You have given me the mind of Christ as a gift of Your grace. You have given me your righteous mind. I hold the thoughts, feelings, and purposes of Your heart toward myself, toward others, and toward the circumstances in my life. Today I embrace that as my true identity and I thank You for changing the way I think by the power of Your Spirit. In Jesus' name, amen.

Reflection and Discussion Questions for Chapter 1

1. What is the main truth that spoke to you in this chapter and how will you apply it in your life?

2. How do we reign in life over every negative circumstance? (Romans 5:17).

3. What is your true identity concerning your mind? (1 Corinthians 2:16).

4. How is the mind of Christ manifested in your thoughts? What powerful truth is revealed in 1 Corinthians 2:11-16?

5. What does 2 Timothy 1:7 reveal about the truth concerning your mind?

6. What does it mean to struggle in your mind? Think about a time when you were struggling with negative thoughts about something in your life. What does Jesus ask us to do when we find ourselves struggling? (Matthew 11:28-30).

7. Read Proverbs 4:23 again. Why do you think it is so important that we embrace our identity in Christ concerning our minds?

8. Have you ever embraced Isaiah 55:7-9 as the truth about you? What did you learn today about the context of those verses? What is the truth about your mind? (1 Corinthians 2:16).

9. Take time today to own the truth about your identity in Christ concerning your mind and thoughts. Talk to Jesus about what you learned today and invite the Holy Spirit to continue to reveal this powerful truth to your heart.

Chapter 2

Let God Change the Way You Think

1 Corinthians 2:16 says, *"...We have the mind of Christ (the Messiah) and do hold the thoughts (feelings and purposes) of His heart"* (AMPC).

We learned in the last chapter that the mind of Christ is our true identity. It's not something we're trying to get, but it's part of our new nature in Jesus. When we became the righteousness of God in Jesus, we were given the mind of Christ as a gift of His grace. 1 Corinthians 2:16 says that we "have" the mind of Christ and do hold the thoughts, feelings and purposes of God's heart.

For many years of my Christian life, I did not experience this truth. Even though I was declared righteous in Jesus and given the mind of Christ as my new nature, I experienced a lot of negative thinking. I thought negatively about myself, and I often had negative thoughts about others. I struggled with doubt, fear, worry, and insecurity in my thoughts. The reason I did not experience the mind of Christ is because I did not embrace it as the truth about who I am in Jesus. In John 8:32, Jesus told us very clearly who would experience freedom in their hearts and minds.

"For if you embrace the truth, it will release more freedom into your lives" (TPT).

We all know that God's thoughts are never negative, depressed, fearful, anxious or ashamed. He is never confused, nor does He experience feelings of guilt or condemnation toward Himself or anyone else. God is love, so His mind is filled with love for everyone. 1 Corinthians 13:4-8 reveals that He doesn't look down on anyone but always believes the best.

So, if we have been given the mind of Christ then why do so many Christians experience these negative thoughts in their minds? Why are so many of God's children depressed, sad, discouraged, fearful, anxious, confused, angry, bitter, judgmental, and even struggling with addictions? Could it be that we haven't fully understood and embraced this truth about our identity? Could it be that we are still trying to think right on our own, instead of relying on the Holy Spirit within us?

I shared in the last chapter about a situation in my own life when I was struggling with fear and worry concerning one of my daughters. We all know that Jesus does not have a worried mind, so I was not experiencing the mind of Christ. If the Scripture says that I have the mind of Christ, why was I experiencing worry instead of peace? Why was I struggling with negative, fearful thoughts? The answer to these questions is so clear in the Word of God.

God's Thoughts Are Only Understood by His Spirit

1 Corinthians 2:11 says, *"After all, who can really see into a person's heart and know his hidden impulses except for that person's spirit? So it is with God. His thoughts and secrets are only fully understood by his Spirit, the Spirit of God"* (TPT).

If the thoughts of God are *only* understood by His Spirit, then that means that I can never experience the mind of Christ by trying to think right in my own human effort. When I was struggling with fearful thoughts, I knew that the Scriptures told me not to worry about anything. But no matter how hard I tried to think right, those worried thoughts kept returning to my mind. I needed power beyond myself.

We've all heard messages on renewing our minds, but if we try to do so in our own ability, we will always struggle to think right. If God's thoughts are only fully understood by His Spirit, human effort just won't do!

1 Corinthians 2:14 says, *"Someone living on an entirely human level rejects the revelations of God's Spirit, for they make no sense to him. He can't understand the revelations of the Spirit because they are only discovered by the illumination of the Spirit"* (TPT).

Someone living entirely on a human level is simply a person who relies upon their own ability to think right thoughts. Embracing the mind of Christ makes no sense to them so they reject this powerful revelation of God's Spirit. When we depend on ourselves, we will never experience the mind of Christ because the thoughts of God are only discovered by the Holy Spirit illuminating our minds with the truth and empowering us to think like God.

We cannot try hard enough to think like God. Apart from Jesus, we can do nothing (John 15:5)! It's the Spirit of God who illuminates our minds with the thoughts, feelings, and purposes of God's heart.

For example, when I embraced the truth that I have the mind of Christ and asked the Holy Spirit to fill my mind with the truth, all of a sudden, the promises of God flooded my mind, and the peace of God rose up in my heart. My perspective of the situation changed, and I could see it through my Father's eyes. I found myself thinking differently by the power of God's Spirit. I remember praying, "Father, You have given me the mind of Christ. I ask you right now to help me think right. Help me to see this situation from Your perspective. I thank You that You have given me the mind of Christ about this situation."

I felt the power of the Holy Spirit working in me, and I began to think differently. I began to experience the mind of Christ in my thoughts.

There Are Two Ways to Live

Romans 8:6 says, *"For the mind-set of the flesh is death, but the mind-set controlled by the Spirit finds life and peace"* (TPT).

Romans 8:6 in the Amplified Bible says, *"Now the mind of the flesh [which is sense and reason without the Holy Spirit] is death... But the mind of the [Holy] Spirit is life and [soul] peace [both now and forever]."*

And Galatians 3:5-6 says, *"Answer this question: Does the God who lavishly provides you with his own presence, his Holy Spirit, working things in your lives you could never do for yourselves, does he do these things because of your strenuous moral striving or because you trust him to do them in you? Don't these things happen among you just as they happened with Abraham? He believed God, and that act of belief was turned into a life that was right with God"* (MSG).

The Galatians had begun their new lives in Christ depending on the Holy Spirit within them, but because of false teaching, they had gone back to living life dependent on their own human effort. The Apostle Paul emphasized to them that it is believing who we are in Jesus and relying upon the Holy Spirit that causes us to experience the life of God.

Now, Romans 8:6 describes two different ways we can live. It says the mindset of the flesh produces death, but the mindset controlled by the Spirit produces life and peace. So, what is the mindset of the flesh? The Amplified Bible describes the mindset of the flesh as sense and reasoning without the Holy Spirit.

It can't get any clearer than that. This means that when I was laying in my bed reasoning in my mind about this situation, worrying on what I could do or say to fix it, I was reasoning without the Holy Spirit, and it was producing death in me. Do you know what death feels like? It feels like fear, anxiety, worry, shame, frustration and anger in your soul. This is not the mind of Christ!

When we reason without the Holy Spirit's help it produces death, but Jesus came to give us His life. He sent the Holy Spirit to be our Comforter, Helper, Strengthener, and to guide us into all truth. He sent Him to help us think right and bring peace to our minds and hearts.

There are so many things in this life that we think about. We think about decisions we need to make. We think about relationships we are in. We think about our children. We think about our finances. We think about our health.

When we reason on these things without the Holy Spirit it produces confusion, fear, and concern. But when we invite the Holy Spirit into our thoughts, He fills our minds with the thoughts, feelings, and purposes of God's heart about our lives.

In The Passion Translation, 1 Corinthians 2:16 says that we possess Christ's perceptions. In other words, when we rely on the Holy Spirit within us, He helps us to see ourselves and others through the eyes of Jesus. We begin to see from His perspective, and that brings life and peace to our souls.

The Holy Spirit Longs to Be Welcome

James 4:5-6 says, *"Or do you suppose that the Scripture is speaking to no purpose that says, The Spirit Whom He has caused to dwell in us yearns over us and He yearns for the Spirit [to be welcome] with a jealous love? But He gives us more and more grace (power of the Holy Spirit, to meet this evil tendency and all others fully). That is why He says, God sets Himself against the proud and haughty, but gives grace [continually] to the lowly (those who are humble enough to receive it)"* (AMPC).

What a powerful scripture! It says the Spirit of God yearns within us to be welcome with a jealous love. It's amazing to me the power God has given us to choose. The Scriptures say that He has set life and death before us, and then He pleads with us to choose life. He says to each of us, *"Oh, that you would choose life, so that you and your descendants might live!"* (Deuteronomy 30:19, NLT).

The Holy Spirit lives within each one of us, but He does not automatically manifest the life of God within our lives. Every day we get to choose whether we will live our lives reasoning without Him or invite Him to bring forth God's life in our thoughts and minds.

In Romans 8:6, those two choices are seen so clearly. We can either live by thinking on our own, reasoning without the Holy Spirit, and experience death in our souls. Or we can choose to invite the Holy Spirit into our thoughts, allowing Him to reveal the truth to us that will set our hearts free to experience His life and peace.

What Is the Grace of God?

2 Corinthians 1:12 says, *"...the grace of God (the unmerited favor and merciful kindness by which God,*

exerting His holy influence upon souls, turns them to Christ, and keeps, strengthens, and increases them in Christian virtues)" (AMPC).

The very grace of God is the Holy Spirit's influence upon our thoughts and minds which empowers us to believe who we are in Christ and brings forth the fruit of God's Spirit in our lives. The Holy Spirit was given to us to empower us to believe! We don't even believe in our own strength! We can let go of our human effort and let Him do the work in us!

Let God Change the Way You Think

Romans 12:2 says, *"Don't copy the behavior and customs of this world, but let God transform you into a new person by changing the way you think. Then you will learn to know God's will for you, which is good and pleasing and perfect"* (NLT).

In The Message, Romans 12:1-2 says, *"So here's what I want you to do, God helping you: Take your everyday, ordinary life—your sleeping, eating, going-to-work, and walking-around life—and place it before God as an offering. Embracing what God does for you is the best thing you can do for him. Don't become so well-adjusted to your culture that you fit into it without even thinking. Instead, fix your attention on God. You'll be changed from the inside out..."*

And The Passion Translation of Romans 12:2 says, *"Stop imitating the ideals and opinions of the culture around you, but be inwardly transformed by the Holy Spirit through a total reformation of how you think. This will empower you to discern God's will as you live a beautiful life, satisfying and perfect in his eyes."*

I especially love how Romans 12:2 reads in the New Living Translation. It says to let God transform your life by

23

changing the way you think. When we ask God to change the way we think, we will learn to know God's good and perfect will and experience it in our lives.

In The Passion Translation, this verse tells us to stop imitating the ideas and opinions of the world around us, but be inwardly transformed by the Holy Spirit through a total reformation of how we think. This will empower you to perceive God's will, and you will live a beautiful and satisfying life. When we let the Holy Spirit transform the way we think, we begin to live a beautiful life filled with His love, joy and peace. Do you want a beautiful life? I know I do! I want the life of Christ manifested in me!

My mind used to be filled with negative thoughts that I wasn't good enough. Thoughts of fear, doubt, and shame brought death to my soul. I lived my life reasoning without the Holy Spirit for many years. But when I began to embrace my true identity in Christ, my thoughts began to change. I began to feel confident, secure, and loved! I began to think about myself differently, and I no longer struggled with a low self-image. I began to believe God like I've never believed God before. I began to believe that I am righteous, favored, and blessed because of Jesus and it came so easily. I truly began to experience a beautiful life, just like the Scriptures promised.

One day I asked the Father, "Why has it become so easy to believe what You say about me, and yet I see so many of my sisters and brothers in Christ still struggling to believe what You say about them?" The Spirit of God said to me so clearly, "Connie, you embraced what I said about you and asked Me to create in you the power and desire to do what pleases Me. You asked Me to help you, and I have empowered you to believe!"

I was in awe as I realized that the Gospel was so simple. Yet so many Christians are still struggling in their own effort to think right and believe right when the Holy Spirit is within them, just waiting for them to embrace their true identity and ask for His help.

Philippians 2:13 says, *"[Not in your own strength] for it is God Who is all the while effectually at work in you [energizing and creating in you the power and desire], both to will and to work for His good pleasure and satisfaction and delight"* (AMPC).

Philippians 2:13 totally changed my life. I remember when the Holy Spirit revealed to me that I didn't have to struggle anymore. Instead, He would create in me the desire and power to carry out God's purpose for my life. I began to pray this verse over myself, continually relying upon Him to strengthen and empower me. I found myself effortlessly thinking differently, believing differently and seeing myself, my husband, and others differently. I didn't realize it at the time, but the Holy Spirit was illuminating my mind with the thoughts of God, and I was experiencing the mind of Christ by the power of the Spirit.

If we've been in church very long, we've heard messages on renewing our minds. It's so important that our minds are renewed, but we must realize this is not a job we must do on our own. It's a work of God's Spirit within us. When we understand that it is God who changes the way we think, when we feel ourselves struggling in our thoughts, we will simply come to the throne of grace to receive God's mercy and grace to remind us who we are in Jesus and help us to think right (Hebrews 4:16).

Proverbs 16:3 says, *"Roll your works upon the Lord [commit and trust them wholly to Him; He will cause your thoughts to become agreeable to His will, and] so shall your plans be established and succeed"* (AMPC).

Do you hear what this verse is saying? It's not you who causes your thoughts to be agreeable to His will, but it's God who causes your thoughts to be agreeable to His will. When you trust Him to do that, your plans will become established and succeed! What a powerful promise from God!

It is God who changes the way we think. Embracing what God does for you is the best thing you can do for Him. When we fix our eyes on Jesus, we are changed from the inside out. When we look to Him and embrace our true identity, and ask Him to change the way we think, He will totally transform the way we think about everything! Then we will be able to discern and understand the thoughts, feelings and purposes of God's heart as we live beautiful lives, satisfying and perfect in His eyes!

Receive God's Grace, Embrace the Mind of Christ, and Reign in Life!

Romans 5:17 says, *"...those who receive [God's] overflowing grace... and the free gift of righteousness... reign as kings in life through the one Man Jesus Christ..."* (AMPC).

"Receive" in this verse is the Greek word *lambano*, which means to "actively lay hold of to take or receive" or "to lay hold by aggressively (actively) accepting what is available (offered). So, if you've been struggling in your mind with confusion, depression, fear, anxiety, guilt or any negative thought toward yourself or someone else, it's time to reign! Look to Jesus and embrace the truth that you have His mind! Rely on the Holy Spirit within you to change the way you think, and you'll find your thoughts and feelings changing from the inside out by His power! You'll begin to experience the beautiful, satisfied life that Jesus came to give you. Remember, the mind of Christ is your true identity! It's time to live free from every negative thought and experience His life of love, joy and peace by the power of His Spirit! This is your inheritance as a beloved child of God!

Reflection and Discussion Questions for Chapter 2

1. What is the main truth that spoke to you in this chapter and how will you apply it to your life?

2. Why do you think so many Christians struggle with doubt, fear, guilt, and negative thoughts about themselves if they've been given the mind of Christ?

3. According to John 8:32, how can you experience freedom from depression, confusion, fear, and all negative thinking?

4. According to 1 Corinthians 2:11 and 14, how do you experience the mind of Christ? Have you ever tried to think right in your own effort? What truth did the Apostle Paul teach us in Galatians 3:5-6?

5. Romans 8:6 explains two different ways we can live. What is the difference between the mind-set of the flesh and the mind-set of the Spirit? Recall a time that you reasoned without the Holy Spirit and how it affected your heart. Now recall a time that you relied on the Holy Spirit within you to think right. How did that affect your heart?

6. The Holy Spirit lives within you. What is the Holy Spirit yearning for? (James 4:5-6).

7. Read Romans 12:2 again. If you allow the Holy Spirit to change the way you think, how will it affect your life?

8. According to Philippians 2:13, when we let go of our own human effort to think right and trust the Holy Spirit within us, what will He produce in our lives?

Take time today to embrace the truth that you have the mind of Christ and invite the Holy Spirit to manifest this truth in your life! He is waiting for you to ask for His help!

Chapter 3

Negative Thoughts are Not Your Thoughts

The truth that I'm going to share in this chapter has the power to radically affect every area of your life! Thoughts are powerful!

Proverbs 4:23 says, *"Be careful how you think; your life is shaped by your thoughts"* (GNT).

Scientists have confirmed that negative thoughts create stress which upsets the body's hormone balance, depletes the brain of chemicals required for happiness, and damages the immune system. We have all felt the effects that negative, fearful thoughts have on our bodies and our minds. Scientists tell us that 87-95% of current mental and physical illness comes from our thought lives.

The effect that thoughts have on your mind and body are a matter of life or death. Negative thoughts are toxic. They create negative emotions that have a negative impact on our minds, relationships, productivity, success, finances, health and self-image. What we experience in this life comes from our thoughts. Proverbs 4:23 tells us that our lives are shaped by our thoughts. Every word we speak, every decision we make, and every action we take begins in our thoughts.

This is why embracing the truth that the mind of Christ is your true identity is imperative to your entire well-being. This truth has the power to bring forth the very life of God in you and cause you to experience life more abundantly!

Let's read this powerful truth once again in 1 Corinthians 2:16: *"For who has known or understood the mind (the counsels and purposes) of the Lord so as to guide and instruct Him and give Him knowledge? But we have the mind of Christ (the Messiah) and do hold the thoughts (feelings and purposes) of His heart"* (AMPC).

Jesus does not have a negative mindset. He does not think negatively about you, your finances, your health, or your future, and He does not think negatively about the people in your life. He's not depressed, confused, anxious, worried or stressed. His mind is filled with love, joy, peace, goodness, faith, and self-control.

All of us are tempted to be stressed, worried, anxious or fearful at times, but this is not who we are—it's not our true identity. Any thought that does not produce the fruit of the Spirit in us is not ours. Since you have the mind of Christ, this means that every negative thought that enters your mind is not your thought. It did not originate from you! So, where do these negative, destructive thoughts come from?

1 Peter 5:8 says, *"Stay alert! Watch out for your great enemy, the devil. He prowls around like a roaring lion, looking for someone to devour"* (NLT).

The word "devour" in this verse actually means to destroy or to overwhelm with sorrow or sadness (blueletterbible.com).

Jesus taught us this same truth. In John 10:10, Jesus said, *"A thief has only one thing in mind—he wants to steal, slaughter, and destroy. But I have come to give you everything in abundance, more than you expect—life in its fullness until you overflow!"* (TPT).

Since scientists have proven that negative thoughts actually have the power to bring destruction to our minds and our bodies, then negative thoughts are obviously what the devil uses to try to bring harm to us and destroy our lives.

It is imperative that we understand that negative thoughts are not our thoughts so that we will be equipped to guard our hearts from every toxic thought that enters our minds. The Scriptures teach us very clearly that when we have negative thoughts, they come from an external source. They don't come from our born-again, true identity. They come from the enemy.

He brings these negative thoughts to your mind in hopes that you will embrace them as your identity so that they will have a negative impact on your life. He wants to destroy your self-image, your health, your marriage, and your relationships. This was his plan for all of God's children from the beginning of time.

The Scriptures make it clear that the devil is influencing the minds of people in the world. John 8:44 says that he is the father of all lies. 2 Corinthians 4:4 tells us that the god of this world has blinded unbelievers minds so that they cannot discern the truth. And 1 John 5:19 says, *"the whole world [around us] is under the power of the evil one"* (AMPC). As believers in Christ, we are encouraged in James 4:7 to *"Resist the devil [stand firm against him], and he will flee from you"* (AMPC).

A Negative Thought Is the Devil Trying to Corrupt Your Mind with Lies

2 Corinthians 11:2-3 says, *"You need to know that God's passion is burning inside me for you, because, like a loving father, I have pledged your hand in marriage to Christ, your true bridegroom. I've also promised that I would present his*

31

fiancée to him as a pure virgin bride. But now I'm afraid that just as Eve was deceived by the serpent's clever lies, your thoughts may be corrupted and you may lose your single-hearted devotion and pure love for Christ" (TPT).

I don't know if this truth can be any clearer. Eve was given the mind of Christ. The Father, Son, and Holy Spirit breathed life into her by speaking over her, "You are just like us! You are good—so very good—and we approve of you completely. You are excellent in every way!" (Genesis 1:27, 31). That was the mind of Christ toward Eve and her true identity! In that moment, she experienced the very life of God. The Bible says her thoughts and heart were free from any fear or shame.

Then the devil came from the outside to corrupt her mind with his lies. Negative thoughts about God, and herself, filled her mind. These thoughts were not her thoughts. They did not originate from her. They came from the voice of death, the enemy of her soul. They were toxic and their purpose was to produce death in her. Eve embraced those negative thoughts as her own and believed the lies of her enemy. As a result, her heart, which was once filled with the life of God, was now filled with death. Fear and shame brought death to her soul.

The exact same thing is still happening in the thoughts of God's children today. The Apostle Paul said, "I have presented you as Christ's pure and holy bride; this is your true identity, but I fear that just like the devil corrupted Eve's thoughts with his lies, he will do the same thing to you."

The devil wants to corrupt your mind from your pure devotion to Jesus. What does it mean to be purely devoted to Jesus? It means to believe Him instead of the lies of the devil. Whoever we let define us is the one to whom we are devoted. Our thoughts are either devoted to the lies of our enemy, or to Jesus, the Lover of our souls. When we embrace the truth that we have the mind of Christ, we are purely devoted to Jesus and His word of truth about us!

The mind of Christ is a mind filled with love, joy, peace, confidence and security. That's the mind Jesus gave us. When we became His bride, He gave us His righteous identity. He gave us His righteous mind, so any negative thought that tries to enter your mind is not your thought. It's the enemy corrupting your thoughts so that you will no longer believe what Jesus says about you and your true identity in Him.

Since I have embraced this powerful truth that negative thoughts are not my thoughts, I have become very aware of any negative thought that enters my mind. Negative thoughts have lost their power in my life! It has become a new level of freedom for me, and I want everyone to experience it!

When the voice of death tries to corrupt my mind with a negative thought about myself or someone else, I simply say, "No! That thought is not my thought, and I refuse to embrace it! I have the mind of Christ!"

If someone offered you poison, would you drink it? I wouldn't! That's how I see negative thoughts: they are toxic. They are designed by the enemy of my soul to destroy my life, and I refuse to drink his poison!

Let me give you a couple of great examples. The other day, a negative thought about my husband entered my mind. Prior to my understanding of the truths I am sharing with you, I may have pondered that thought and become frustrated with him for a while—but not this day!

I caught that toxic, accusing, negative thought as soon as it entered my mind, and replied, "Not today, devil! That is not my thought! I have the mind of Christ, and I only think positive, loving thoughts about my husband!" I then began to pray for my husband. I found myself thanking God that

33

my husband had the mind of Christ, and peace and love rose up in my heart toward him. Can you imagine the effect this truth can have on marriages? If every husband and wife embraced the truth that they have the mind of Christ toward their spouse, the devil would lose his power to destroy marriages with his toxic thoughts!

Since I began to embrace the mind of Christ as my true identity, I am keenly aware that every negative or fearful thought that enters my mind—about my finances, my friends, myself, my husband, my future, my business, my ministry, and my life—is not my thought! They come from the outside for one reason: to bring destruction to my life and keep me from fulfilling God's plan for my life.

Another area of my life that has been dramatically affected by this truth is in my thoughts about time and projects I want to do. Every one of us deal with the issue of time. We all have many things we want to get done each day. Quite often, when I'd have a lot of things to do, these thoughts would come to my mind: *I don't have enough time. I don't know how to get this done. I can't do this.*

I recognized that these negative thoughts were causing me to be unfocused, and they were adversely affecting the productivity of my day. I would procrastinate doing things that were in my heart to do because these lies had corrupted my mind, and I had believed them.

But since I had become aware that negative thoughts are not my thoughts, and that they are designed to destroy the dreams in my heart, that day I stopped and said, "These thoughts are not my thoughts! Jesus, what do You think about this? Since I have Your mind, what are Your thoughts about my time?"

The Holy Spirit illuminated my mind with this simple truth. He said, "I have made 24 hours in each day. I have given you plenty of time in each day, and I have equipped you with everything you need to accomplish what I have planned for you to do today."

He also revealed that I had been embracing the false identity of a procrastinator and that it was not the truth about me. I am one with Jesus, and He finishes what He starts. That is the mind of Christ about me! I have plenty of time! I can do all things through Christ who strengthens me! And I am a finisher of every project Jesus puts in my heart!

Since that revelation came to me concerning the mind of Christ, I have found myself so much more focused, creative, and productive each day. Things that I've had on my heart to get done for years were accomplished in a very short period of time! It truly was amazing to see how negative thoughts really had hindered me from accomplishing the dreams and desires of my heart. Yet, when I realized that those negative thoughts are not my thoughts, and refused to tolerate them, they lost their power in my life.

Ephesians 6:16-17 says, *"In every battle, take faith as your wrap-around shield, for it is able to extinguish the blazing arrows coming at you from the Evil One! Embrace the power of salvation's full deliverance, like a helmet to protect your thoughts from lies..."* (TPT).

In these verses, we see once again that negative thoughts come at us from the outside. They are blazing arrows that come at you from the evil one. But when we embrace the power of salvation's full deliverance, it protects our minds from the enemy's lies.

How do you embrace the power of salvation's full deliverance? You do that by embracing your true identity in Christ and declaring what is true about you. Declare the truth right now: "I am the righteousness of God in Christ Jesus! Negative thoughts are not my thoughts! I have the mind of Christ!"

35

When you understand that negative thoughts are not your thoughts, you won't take ownership of them. They will lose their power to condemn you or make you feel guilty.

Romans 8:1 says, *"So now the case is closed. There remains no accusing voice of condemnation against those who are joined in life-union with Jesus, the Anointed One"* (TPT).

The case is closed! You have the mind of Christ. Any negative thought is the accusing voice of condemnation. And this verse says that there remains no more accusing voice of condemnation against you because you are one with Jesus! You have His mind!

Negative thoughts come at us all! If you believe that the negative thoughts that enter your mind come from you, they will have the power to condemn you. Have you ever had a negative thought enter your mind and then the next thought you had was, *How could I think like that? What's wrong with me?* I know I have. But not anymore! Now that I know that negative thoughts are not my thoughts, I will not be duped by that lie ever again.

When you understand this powerful truth, you won't tolerate negative thoughts in your mind. When a negative thought comes at you about **yourself**, you'll respond, "Not today, devil! That's not my thought! I have the mind of Christ!"

When a negative thought comes at you about **your life**, you'll respond, "Not today, devil! That's not my thought! I have the mind of Christ!"

When a negative thought comes at you about **someone else**, you'll respond, "Not today, devil! That's not my thought! I have the mind of Christ!" The negative, toxic, accusing thoughts of the devil will have truly lost their power to condemn you, and you will truly begin to reign in life!

2 Corinthians 10:5 says, *"...We capture, like prisoners of war, every thought and insist that it bow in obedience to the Anointed One"* (TPT).

Above Everything You Do, Guard Your Heart From Toxic Thoughts!

Proverbs 4:23 says, *"Guard your heart above all else, for it determines the course of your life"* (NLT).

The word "heart" in this verse means "the mind, the thoughts, the feelings and emotions of a man" (Strong's H3820). This verse tells us that the most important thing you can do is guard your mind and thoughts. Every thought will either produce life or death.

You can know immediately if thoughts are from the Spirit within you, or the enemy of your soul, by how they make you feel. Our emotions are good indicators of whether we are being presented with the truth or a lie! Lies put us in bondage to fear, guilt, shame, and anger, and they produce anxiety and stress! But the truth sets us free to experience the life of God within us, which is love, joy, and peace.

Listen to what your good Father has spoken to your heart in Proverbs 4:10: *"My son, if you will take the time to stop and listen to me and embrace what I say, you will live a long and happy life full of understanding in every way"* (TPT).

Did you hear what your good Father promised you in this verse? He promised that if you would simply take the time to stop and listen to Him, and embrace what He says about you, you'll experience a long and happy life, full of understanding in every way. I love that! What did your good Father say to you in 1 Corinthians 2:16? He said you have the mind of Christ! If you will take hold of that truth and reject any negative, toxic thought to the contrary, you'll experience the fullness of life that Jesus came to give you!

Now, listen to what your good Father says to you in Proverbs 4:20-23: *"My child, pay attention to my words; listen closely to what I say. Don't ever forget my words; keep them always in mind. They are the key to life for those who find them; they bring health to the whole body. Be careful what you think, because your thoughts run your life"* (NCV).

While the voice of death—negative thoughts—has the power to destroy your life, the voice of your good Father has the power to bring forth life and health to your whole body. Today your good Father is speaking to your heart. This is what He is saying, "My child, guard your mind from every negative thought! Those thoughts are not your thoughts! Remember, you have the mind of Christ! Embrace what I say about you!"

So, the next time a negative, accusing, fearful thought enters your mind, boldly respond, "Not today, devil! That is not my thought! I believe what my good Father says about me! I have the mind of Christ!"

Reflection and Discussion Questions for Chapter 3

1. What is the main truth that spoke to you in this chapter and how will you apply it to your life?

2. Have you ever felt the effects of negative, fearful thoughts in your body? What has science proven about how negative thoughts affect our lives, and why is it vitally important that we pay attention to what we are thinking? (Proverbs 4:23).

3. What does the devil use to destroy our lives? If negative thoughts are not your thoughts, where do negative, accusing thoughts come from? (2 Corinthians 11:2-4).

4. How can you protect your thoughts from the enemy's lies? What does it mean to embrace salvation's full deliverance? (Ephesians 6:16-17).

5. What did your good Father promise you in Proverbs 4:10?

6. When you listen to the voice of death, what will it produce in your heart and life? (John 10:10). What will listening to and embracing what your good Father says about you produce in your life? (Proverbs 4:20-23).

7. How will you respond the next time a negative thought enters your mind? What has your good Father spoken over you concerning your thoughts? What's the truth about your mind?

    Let's declare the truth together!

    "Negative thoughts are not my thoughts! I have the mind of Christ!"

Chapter 4

Jesus Gave You a Brand-New Mind!

1 Corinthians 2:16 says that you have the mind of Christ and do hold the thoughts, feelings and purposes of His heart (AMPC).

Did you know that when you became one with Jesus in His death, burial, and resurrection, you were given a brand-new mind? You became a new creation in Jesus! You were given the very mind of Christ! This scripture says you possess His thoughts, His feelings, and the purposes of His heart within your mind!

What happened in the resurrection of Jesus is so powerful that it not only changed your spirit, but it also changed your mind. Some believe that the born-again experience only affected our spirits, but that our minds were not changed. I have heard it taught that your spirit was saved, but your mind was not, but a closer look at the Scriptures reveals that you were given a brand-new mind in Christ.

When we believe that our minds were not redeemed, we enter into self-effort concerning our thought life, constantly working on thinking right and renewing our minds by our own human effort. We subconsciously have believed that there is nothing wrong with our spirits, but that there is definitely something wrong with our minds, so we need to fix them. This could not be further from the truth. Salvation changed our entire being!

2 Corinthians 5:17 says, *"Therefore, if anyone is in Christ, he is a new creation; old things have passed away; behold, all things have become new"* (NKJV).

This Scripture doesn't say we are new spirits, it says we became entirely new creations. Jesus fully redeemed our entire being when He died and rose again. He redeemed our minds. The Scriptures teach very clearly that He purchased our freedom from depression, shame, worry, fear, and condemnation by giving us a brand-new, righteous identity in Him (Deuteronomy 28:65-67; Galatians 3:13-14). In the born-again experience, we were given the mind of Christ when the Spirit of God came to live inside of us!

In John 14:27 Jesus said, *"I am leaving you with a gift— peace of mind and heart"* (NLT).

Jesus left us with a gift that He paid for with His very life. That gift is peace of mind! WOW! The word "peace" in this verse means "security; safety; prosperity; felicity; rest; to set at one again" (blueletterbible.com, Strong's G1515).

Let's look at John 14:27 with these definitions of peace in mind. Jesus said, "I am leaving you with a gift—a secure, safe, and prosperous mind." Felicity is a mind filled with intense happiness; joyfulness; bliss; euphoria; delight; cheerfulness; satisfaction; and fulfillment.

Let's look at another verse that reveals this same truth. When you became a new creation in Christ Jesus, read what your good Father said He gave you:

In Ezekiel 36:26-27, He said, *"I will give you a new heart and put a new spirit within you; and I will remove the heart of stone from your flesh and give you a heart of flesh.*

I will put My Spirit within you and cause you to walk in My statutes..." (NASB).

The word "heart" in this scripture comes from the Hebrew word *leb*, and it means "the mind; thinking; understanding; the seat of emotions; feelings, the will and even the intellect of a person" (Strong's H3820; blueletterbible.com).

Now let's read these verses again, inserting the definition of "heart" to get a deeper understanding of what Jesus gave us in our new created being.

"I will give you a new mind, a new way of thinking, new understanding, new emotions and feelings, new desires, and even a new intellect; and I will put a new spirit within you; I will remove your heart of stone and give you a heart of flesh. I will put My Spirit within you and cause you to walk in My ways!"

What glorious Good News! When we became new creations in Christ Jesus, we were given a brand-new mind— an entirely new way of thinking by the power of the Spirit.

Let's look at two more translations of these verses.

Ezekiel 36:26 in the Living Bible says, *"And I will give you a new heart—I will give you new and right desires—and put a new spirit within you. I will take out your stony hearts of sin and give you new hearts of love."*

The New Century Version says, *"...I will put a new way of thinking inside you..."* (Ezekiel 36:26).

Your good Father has put a new way of thinking inside you by giving you the very mind of Christ. He has given you a new good heart with new and right desires and put a new spirit within you. He took away your stony heart (sinful nature) and gave you a new heart of love (a brand-new, righteous nature).

This same promise to the New Covenant believer in Christ is also found in Hebrews 8:10. It says, *"For this is the covenant that I will make with the house of Israel after those days, says the Lord: I will imprint My laws upon their minds [even upon their innermost thoughts and understanding] And engrave them upon their hearts [effecting their regeneration]. And I will be their God, And they shall be My people"* (AMP).

We see this truth again in Hebrews 10:16: *"This is the covenant that I will make with them after those days, says the Lord: I will put My laws into their hearts, and in their minds I will write them"* (NKJV).

What laws did God promise to put in our minds and thoughts and understanding?

Romans 8:1-2 tells us, *"Therefore, there is now no condemnation for those who are in Christ Jesus, because through Christ Jesus the law of the Spirit who gives life has set you free from the law of sin and death"* (NIV).

There are two laws in operation. The Old Covenant laws written on stone produced condemnation and death in the heart of man. But the New Covenant law of the Spirit of life in Christ Jesus produces life and peace in the heart of man. The law of the Spirit of life is our brand-new identity in Christ. Our good Father has written on our minds and hearts that we are His beloved children—righteous, holy, good, blessed and favored—because we are one with Jesus! He has removed the spirit of fear and given you a sound mind in Christ.

You've Been Given a Sound Mind in Christ

2 Timothy 1:7 says, *"For God has not given us a spirit of fear, but of power and of love and of a sound mind"* (NKJV).

2 Timothy 1:7 in the Amplified Bible says, *"For God did not give us a spirit of timidity (of cowardice, of craven and cringing and fawning fear), but [He has given us a spirit] of power and of love and of calm and well-balanced mind and discipline and self-control"* (AMPC).

So, what is a calm and well-balanced mind? Calmness is "the state or quality of being free from agitation or strong emotion; The state or condition of being free from disturbance or violent activity" (https://www.lexico.com/en/definition/calmness). Synonyms of the world calmness include tranquility and peace (https://www.thesaurus.com/browse/calmness?s=t). Well-balanced means: "emotionally or psychologically untroubled" (https://www.merriam-webster.com/dictionary/well-balanced).

The Amplified Bible describes a well-balanced mind as discipline and self-control, which is a fruit of the spirit. The mind given to you by the Spirit is free from all addictions. You have a sound, calm, well-balanced mind in Christ!

This is the mind that Jesus paid such a great price to give you! He gave you a mind that is free from agitation, frustration, and disturbance. He gave you an emotionally and psychologically untroubled mind. Your mind has been redeemed and fear has no more power in your life!

The word "sound" comes from the word *sophron* (*sozo*, "to save" and *phren,* "the mind"), and it means, "saving the mind" (See Vine's Expository Dictionary Entry at https://www.blueletterbible.org/lang/lexicon/lexicon.cfm?Strongs=G4995).

You have a saved mind! You've been saved from fear, anxiety and shame. You have the mind of Christ. This is your true identity. You are powerful. You are loved. You have a sound mind because you are one with Jesus! Embrace your true identity in Christ! The Spirit of God defines you!

If this is true, then why do many Christians struggle with fearful thoughts, addictions, depression, and stress? If our minds were made new, then why do some Christians struggle with anxiety and fear?

Have you ever had anxious thoughts overwhelm you, making it difficult to make decisions? Anxiety can lead to overthinking, which makes you more anxious, which leads to more overthinking, and so on. How can you get out of this vicious cycle? Repressing anxious thoughts won't work; they will just pop up again, sometimes with more intensity. Jesus came to set you free from anxious thoughts and give you a sound mind. But how do we experience that truth in our lives?

Every part of our identity in Christ manifests in our lives the exact same way!

2 Corinthians 1:20 says, *"For all of God's promises find their "yes" of fulfillment in him. And as his "yes" and our "amen" ascend to God, we bring him glory!"* (TPT).

The NIV reads, *"For no matter how many promises God has made, they are "Yes" in Christ. And so through him the "Amen" is spoken by us to the glory of God."*

2 Corinthians 1:20 tells us that the "Yes" to all of God's promises are fulfilled in Christ. That means that His promises define who you already are! They describe your new creation in Christ. But the rest of that verse says that the "AMEN" is spoken by us to the glory of God!

This means that God's promises have been fulfilled in Christ. You have a brand-new mind. But in order for you to experience the manifestation of your new identity, you get to decide whether or not you will say, "Amen" to them.

Romans 5:17 tells us that those who receive God's overflowing grace and free gift of righteousness will reign in life through Christ Jesus! Those who reject this truth won't experience it, even though it's true of every believer in Christ.

Those who receive it will experience the peace that passes all understanding as they experience their true identity of a sound, well-balanced mind!

It's time to give up the lie that your mind was not redeemed, and begin to declare the truth about your thoughts and your mind. Embrace your true identity in Christ and declare it to be true in your life!

James 1:21 says, *"...in a humble (gentle, modest) spirit receive and welcome the Word which implanted and rooted [in your hearts] contains the power to save your souls"* (AMPC).

Let's continue to verse 22 in The Passion Translation. It reads, *"Don't just listen to the Word of Truth and not respond to it, for that is the essence of self-deception. So always let his Word become like poetry written and fulfilled by your life!"*

These verses are so clear about who will actually experience the freedom that comes from embracing the truth that we have the mind of Christ. Your good Father has revealed this powerful truth to you in His word. Don't just listen to the Word of Truth and not respond to it, for that is the essence of self-deception. Let the truth that you have a brand-new mind become like poetry upon your heart, fulfilled in your life!

In a humble spirit, receive and welcome this truth about your identity in Christ because it has the power to save your soul. It has the power to save your mind, your will, and your emotions! Jesus came to save your mind from fear, worry, anxiety, shame, guilt and condemnation! Receive the truth and live free in His love!

Ephesians 4:21-24 says, *"Since you have heard about Jesus and have learned the truth that comes from him, throw off your old sinful nature and your former way of life, which is corrupted by lust and deception. Instead, let the Spirit renew your thoughts and attitudes. Put on your new nature, created to be like God—truly righteous and holy"* (NLT).

Ephesians 4:23-24 in The Passion Translation says, *"Now it's time to be made new by every revelation that's been given to you. And to be transformed as you embrace the glorious Christ-within as your new life and live in union with him! For God has re-created you all over again in his perfect righteousness..."*

So, what does it look like to embrace the glorious Christ-within as your new life and live in union with Him? When you find yourself tempted to be anxious, stressed, or worried, take a moment to sit down and focus on Jesus. Remember, what is true about your mind! Come to the throne of grace and say, "Father, I know you love me! Thank You for giving me a sound, well-balanced mind. I have the mind of Christ. I trust You to manifest this truth in my thoughts right now."

Let the Holy Spirit do His job and rest in His ability within you. The peace that passes all understanding will guard your heart and mind as you live in Christ Jesus! (Philippians 4:7).

The wonderful Good News of the Gospel is that your entire being (spirit, soul, and body) has been redeemed and is completely flawless in Christ! But don't take my word for it; read it for yourself!

1 Thessalonians 5:23 says, *"Now, may the God of peace and harmony set you apart, making you completely holy. And may your **entire being**—spirit, soul, and body—be kept completely flawless in the appearing of our Lord Jesus, the Anointed One"* (TPT, emphasis added).

Your *entire being* is completely flawless in Christ! You are not only healed and whole in your spirit, but you are healed and whole in your mind and your body! *Completely flawless!* There's **nothing** wrong with you! Jesus redeemed and restored your *entire being,* and He will keep your spirit, soul, and body completely flawless until the day of His return!

Excuse me for a moment while I do a happy dance! Isn't that the best news you have ever heard? You don't have to put up with fear, worry, anxiety, confusion, guilt or shame for one more moment in your life! You've been given the mind of Christ!

Take a moment right now to embrace Christ within you as your new life and live in union with Him. Speak what is true about your mind! Say, "Yes and Amen" to your new identity in Jesus and let the Holy Spirit manifest it in your life!

"Fear, confusion, guilt, shame, anxiety, and worry: you have no power over me! I am one with Jesus! I've been given an entirely brand-new mind! I have the gift of peace of mind! I have a sound mind in Jesus! I have the very mind of Christ, and I hold His thoughts, His feelings, and the purposes of His heart! Peace, joy, love, confidence and security define my new mind in Christ!"

Reflection and Discussion Questions for Chapter 4

1. What is the main truth that spoke to you in this chapter and how will you apply it to your life?

2. What gift did Jesus say He gave to you in John 14:27 and what does it mean?

3. Read Ezekiel 36:26-27 again. What is the meaning of "heart" in this Scripture, and what did your good Father promise you in these verses?

4. What does 2 Timothy 1:7 say God has given you? What does it mean to have a sound mind?

5. How do we experience the promise of a sound mind that God has given us? (2 Corinthians 1:20).

6. When you are experiencing fear, confusion, shame, or guilt in your mind, what does Ephesians 4:21-24 encourage you to do? Give an example of what it looks like to apply these verses in your life.

7. What Good News about your entire new-created being was revealed in 1 Thessalonians 5:23?

Chapter 5

The Mind of Christ is the
Mind of Perfect Love

1 Corinthians 2:16: *"...We have the mind of Christ (the Messiah) and do hold the thoughts (feelings and purposes) of His heart"* (AMPC).

I just love this scripture! The revelation of our identity in Christ contained in this verse is so powerful! Any negative thought of depression, offense, anxiety, discouragement, confusion, guilt or lack loses its power to define us when we lay hold of this truth about our identity.

You have the mind of Christ! You hold the thoughts, the feelings and the purposes of God's heart in your thoughts and mind. You learned in a previous chapter that the word "have" in this verse means "to possess; to lay hold of; to take ownership of; to own." So often, if we read a verse like this but aren't experiencing it, we tend to think, *I need to get that. I need to ponder that more so I can really understand it. I still struggle with negative thoughts, so how can that be true about me?* We define ourselves by our experience, instead of simply laying hold of and taking ownership of what our good Father says about us in Christ.

53

When you own the mind of Christ, and believe that you hold the thoughts, feelings and purposes of God's heart, you will find your mind free from any negative thoughts about yourself or others. You will begin to love yourself and others with the love of Jesus by the power of God's Spirit.

Jesus doesn't have any negative thoughts about you or anyone else, and since you have the mind of Christ, neither do you! Any negative thought that enters your mind about yourself or someone else is not your thought! It's from the enemy of your soul, and the purpose of those negative thoughts is to destroy your life and your relationships. Remember, negative thoughts about yourself and others are toxic to your mental and physical well-being. When you understand that truth, you won't tolerate those negative thoughts for one more moment in your life.

2 Timothy 1:7 says, *"For God has not given us a spirit of fear, but of power and of love and of a sound mind"* (NKJV).

God has given us a spirit of love! In The Living Bible, Ezekiel 36:26 says, *"I will give you a new heart—I will give you new and right desires—and put a new spirit within you. I will take out your stony hearts of sin and give you new hearts of love."*

1 John 4:16 tells us that God is love! That means that the mind of Christ is the mind of love!

Jesus Gave You a New Mind of Love

What is the mind of love? How does Jesus think and feel toward you and others?

1 Corinthians 13:4-8 clearly answers this question. If you have been in church very long, I'm sure you are familiar with this passage of Scripture that describes what love is. Love is

the one word that perfectly defines the nature and character of God. So, if we want to know the mind of Christ—if we want to understand the thoughts, feelings, and purposes of God's heart—then all we have to do is read this passage of Scripture that defines love.

As we read these verses, we will gain a deeper understanding that the mind of Christ is the mind of love. We are one with Jesus. We have His mind toward ourselves and everyone else in our lives. We are not trying to walk in love; it's who we are!

I've taken 1 Corinthians 13:4-8 from many translations of the Bible to get the clearest and best understanding of love. Let's read this paraphrase of verses 4-5 together:

"Love is patient and kind. Love is never envious, nor does it boil over with jealousy. Love is not conceited or inflated with pride; it is not snobbish, nor does it cherish ideas of its own importance. Love does not look down on others. Love does not judge, criticize or condemn others."

The Mind of Christ Is Patient and Kind

Your good Father is never angry, disappointed, or frustrated with you. He only has thoughts of loving-kindness and compassion. He is always patient with you (Isaiah 54:9-10). The mind of love is patient and kind. Those are the thoughts and feelings of God's heart toward you.

Since you have the mind of Christ, you hold the thoughts and feelings of His heart toward yourself as well. We have all felt angry, disappointed and frustrated with ourselves or someone else at times. But when we understand that those thoughts are not our thoughts, we can reject them, and say, "Father, I have the mind of Christ. Those thoughts and feelings are not mine! I am one with You! I am patient and kind, just like You. Empower me by Your Spirit to see myself and others through your eyes." It's in these moments of frustration, or when we are feeling impatient, that we take a moment to invite the Holy Spirit into our thoughts to bring His peace to our minds. He is an ever-present help in time of need (Psalm 46:1).

The Mind of Christ Is Never Jealous of Others

Can you imagine Jesus being jealous of you? That sounds ridiculous, doesn't it? Why would the Son of God, who sits in the place of highest honor, be jealous of anyone?

Jealous thoughts are not in the mind of Christ because He knows He is one with the Father, and He is complete in Him! Since you are one with Him, you have a mind that is never envious of others either—the mind of Christ.

I remember when I used to be jealous of others. It was something I really struggled with. I can remember thinking, *I wish I had what they had. Why is that happening for them, but not for me?* At the time, I did not know my identity in Christ. I saw myself as lacking and believed they were more blessed than me.

But as I began to see myself as one with Jesus, seated in the highest position of honor in Him, and blessed with every blessing in Christ, I began to experience the mind of Christ and jealous thoughts lost their power in my life.

When jealous thoughts try to enter your mind, remember, those thoughts are not your thoughts. You have the mind of Christ! You are one with the King of kings. You are blessed with every spiritual blessing in Christ, and you lack nothing (Ephesians 1:3)! If you sit in the highest place of honor in the heavenly realm as one with Jesus, why would you be jealous of anyone?

The Mind of Christ Is Not Inflated with Pride

The mind of love is not conceited or inflated with pride. Jesus does not think of Himself as superior or better than you! WOW! He is the King of kings, and yet He humbled Himself and became the Son of Man so that the sons of men could become sons of God. He gave us His glory and made us one with Him. He gave us His perfect righteousness as our new identity in Him (John 17:20-26). That's the mind of Christ. In Christ, we are all equally loved, equally righteous, and equally blessed!

The truth is, none of our good works makes us better than anyone else. We are good because Jesus gave us His perfect righteousness as a gift of His grace. Jesus sees all of His beautiful brides in the exact same way.

Jesus shared His thoughts and mind toward us all in Song of Songs 4:7: *"My darling, everything about you is beautiful, and there is nothing at all wrong with you"* (NCV).

If we embraced what Jesus said about us as the truth, would we ever feel superior or better than anyone else? No, pride would lose its power in our lives. The truth about you is that you have the mind of Christ! Whenever a thought of being better than someone else enters your mind, remember that it is not your thought. Invite the Holy Spirit to change the way you think and illuminate your mind with the truth. You'll begin to see yourself and others through the eyes of perfect love.

The Mind of Christ Doesn't Judge, Criticize or Condemn

If God is love, then your Heavenly Father never looks down on you. He does not judge you, criticize you or condemn you. That's the mind of perfect love. You have the mind of Christ. You hold His thoughts and feelings toward yourself and others. That means you do not look down on yourself. You do not judge, criticize, or condemn yourself or anyone else.

Listen to the mind of Christ toward you in Romans 4:8: *"What happy progress comes to them when they hear the Lord speak over them, 'I will never hold your sins against you!'"* (TPT).

Your good Father will never hold your sins against you. He will never define you by your sins or bad behavior. He always sees you through eyes of perfect love. Even when you've done wrong, He never changes His opinion of you. He always sees you as righteous, perfect and without fault in His eyes because you are one with Him. That's the mind of perfect love (Ephesians 1:4).

You have the mind of Christ. That means you do not hold your sins against yourself. You do not define yourself by your failures. You define yourself as righteous, perfect and without fault in your Father's eyes because you are one with Jesus.

The same thing is true about others. Since you have the mind of Christ toward others, you don't hold a person's sins or mistakes against them either. You don't define them by their bad behavior. You see them through the eyes of perfect love.

Romans 8:1 says, *"So now the case is closed. There remains no accusing voice of condemnation against those who are joined in life-union with Jesus, the Anointed One"* (TPT). The case is closed! You have the mind of Christ. You've been resurrected to a brand-new life, and that life does not include negative, accusing thoughts about yourself or others.

Just the other day a negative thought entered my mind about a friend of mine. I'm able to admit this because I recognize that this thought was not my thought, and it does not define who I am. That thought was toxic. It was coming from the enemy of my soul for one purpose—to destroy my relationship with my friend. But I caught that thought and made it bow to the resurrected life of Jesus in me!

I remember saying, "That is not my thought! I have the mind of Christ! Jesus, I hold Your thoughts, feelings and the purposes of Your heart toward my friend. Holy Spirit, I invite You right now to illuminate my mind with Your thoughts and feelings toward her." I felt my thoughts changing by the Spirit as I began to think on that which is good and true about her.

I began to pray, "Father, I thank You that I have Your mind toward her and she has Your mind toward me. We see the best in each other because we are one with You!" What peace filled my soul as the mind of Christ filled my thoughts and heart. I felt such love in my heart toward my friend because I have the mind of perfect love by the power of God's Spirit.

Can you imagine the difference this could make in every relationship in our lives? If every time a critical, accusing thought entered our minds, we invited the Holy Spirit to illuminate our thoughts with the truth, perfect love and perfect peace would be the fruit of our lives. Healing and restoration would come to our relationships. We'd experience the good, acceptable, and perfect will of God for our lives.

What's the Mind of Christ Toward the World?

2 Corinthians 5:19 says: *"For God was in Christ, reconciling the world to himself, no longer counting people's sins against them. And he gave us this wonderful message of reconciliation"* (NLT).

This verse makes it very clear that the mind and thoughts of God toward the world is that He is no longer counting any of their sins against them. He has invited us all to share this Good news with the world.

In John 8:1-11, we read a perfect example of this truth in the story of the woman caught in adultery. In this story, Jesus clearly revealed to us the thoughts, feelings and purposes of His heart toward those who are caught in sin. The religious leaders of the day were looking down on this woman. They were judging, criticizing and condemning her with the law. Accusing voices were all around her. But what was the mind of Christ toward her? Perfect love looked at her in the middle of her greatest failure and said, "I do not condemn you!" (John 8:11). Why did He not condemn her? Because perfect love does not judge, criticize, or condemn anyone! He didn't hold her sins against her. Perfect love set her free!

After Jesus set that precious woman free from the condemnation in her own heart and the condemnation coming from the religious leaders, He turned toward them again and made His mind, His thoughts, and His heart very clear! In John 8:15, Jesus said to them, *"You [set yourselves up to] judge according to the flesh (by what you see). [You condemn by external, human standards.] I do not [set Myself up to] judge or condemn or sentence anyone"* (AMP).

What a beautiful picture of the mind of perfect love! That's the mind of Christ! Jesus doesn't judge anyone by external human standards. He doesn't think like the religious world thinks. He came to heal the broken hearted and set the captives free, not to condemn them (John 3:16-17).

So, the next time you have a negative, judgmental, critical, or condemning thought come into your mind, remember that is not your thought. You have the mind of Christ! You have the mind of perfect love! You hold His thoughts, feelings and the purposes of His heart. You don't judge, condemn or sentence anyone! Invite the Holy Spirit to help you see yourself and others through the eyes of perfect love and live the glorious, resurrected life that Jesus came to give you.

Take time right now to embrace and declare the truth that you have the mind of perfect love and invite the Holy Spirit to bring forth that fruit in your life:

Father, today I embrace the truth that I have the mind of Christ, and the mind of Christ is the mind of perfect love. I am one with Jesus! I am patient and kind. I am never envious nor do I boil over with jealousy. I am not conceited or inflated with pride. I am not snobbish, nor do I cherish ideas of my own importance. I do not look down on others, nor do I judge, criticize or condemn others. Any thought that enters my mind that is contrary to this truth is not my thought. I ask you, Holy Spirit, to illuminate my thoughts so that I see myself and others through the eyes of perfect love! In Jesus' name, amen!

Reflection and Discussion Questions for Chapter 5

1. What is the main truth that spoke to you in this chapter and how will you apply it to your life?

2. If God is Love, what is the mind of Christ? How does Ezekiel 36:26-27 describe our new heart?

3. What is the mind of love? How does perfect love think and feel toward people? (1 Corinthians 13:4-7). What is true about you if you are one with perfect love?

4. Read Romans 4:8 again. What does this verse reveal about the mind of Christ toward you and others?

5. What are Jesus' thoughts and feelings toward a person who has sinned? (John 8:15).

6. What is the mind of Christ toward the world? (2 Corinthians 5:19).

7. When negative thoughts come into your mind about yourself or others, how can you experience the mind of Christ instead?

Chapter 6

The Mind of Christ Believes the Best About Every Person

In this chapter, we will continue to understand that the mind of Christ is the mind of perfect love. God is love! 1 Corinthians 13:4-8 describes love. It paints a beautiful picture of the thoughts, feelings and purposes of God's heart toward you and others. Since you have been given His very mind, this passage of Scripture also describes who you are in Christ and how your new nature thinks toward yourself and others.

The Mind of Christ Refuses to Take Offense

1 Corinthians 13:5:

"Love does not offend people by rudeness or being inconsiderate or indecent or rash. It is always courteous. Love (God's love in us) does not insist on its own rights or its own way, for it is not self-seeking. Love is not touchy or fretful or resentful. Love is not easily provoked or prone to anger. It pitches no tantrums and refuses to take offense. Love is not irritable. Love takes no account

of the evil done to it, holds no grudges, does not remember wrongs done to it; does not nurse hurt feelings" (paraphrased from various translations of the Bible).

When we embrace the truth that negative thoughts are not our thoughts, we will reject any negative thought of irritation, frustration, selfishness, resentment, anger, or offense toward others that enters our minds. That's not who we are, and it's not the life Jesus came to give us! Scripture actually teaches us that these negative attitudes and feelings come from the enemy of our soul (Ephesians 4:20-30). These are the moments when we boldly say, "Not today, devil! I have the mind of Christ and I hold His thoughts, feelings and the purposes of His heart toward every person in my life!" We have the mind of Christ and we take no account of wrongs done to us, hold no grudges, and we do not nurse hurt feelings.

There have been many times in my life when I have nursed hurt feelings and taken offense toward someone who did me wrong. These were times when I reasoned without the Holy Spirit and it brought death to my soul. I felt unloved and unappreciated, and it negatively affected relationships in my life. I'm sure you can relate to thinking upon how someone's words or actions upset you and caused you to have a negative opinion of them. When we hold someone's wrong behavior against them, it causes us to build a wall between us and that person, and we are actually coming into agreement with our enemy and His plan to destroy relationships.

Now that I have become aware that nursing hurt feelings is not the mind of Christ, I realize that those thoughts are not my thoughts. Thinking upon how someone hurt me is actually the enemy of my soul trying to poison my mind with his toxic, negative thoughts to bring destruction to my life.

When we become aware of this, we can immediately turn our minds toward Jesus, invite the Holy Spirit into our thoughts, and ask Him to help us see this person from His perspective. This brings life and peace to our minds and our relationships.

What Was Jesus's Mind Toward the Ones Who Did Him Wrong?

When Jesus was hanging upon the cross, His enemies were mocking Him. They had just beaten him, put a crown of thorns on his head, and stripped Him naked. The people He loved were killing Him. In that very moment, we see clearly the mind of Christ toward those who did Him wrong. He said, "Father, forgive them, for they know not what they do!" That is the mind of perfect love and we have been given that mind. It's not something we are trying to get. It's not an attitude we know we should have, but don't. That's the lie the enemy of your soul wants you to believe about yourself.

But the Spirit of God says, "You have the mind of Christ! You hold the thoughts, feelings and purposes of My heart toward every person who has ever done you wrong. That's who you are in Jesus!" Not only does the Spirit of God remind us who we are, but He empowers us to reflect the nature of Christ in this world. He is the One Who brings forth the fruit of love in our thoughts and our lives. By His grace, we are able to look at the people who have done us wrong and with love and compassion say, "Father, show them the truth that will set them free!" That's what true freedom in Christ looks like. It's the mind of perfect love manifested in our lives.

Just like Jesus did, we can actually find our lives in every word our Father says about us. We are loved! We are valuable! We are the delight of His heart! We have His mind!

When we own that as our true identity, those negative words and actions toward us will no longer have any power in our lives. They won't be able to control our emotions nor define who we are. We will live free from every negative thought and every negative feeling toward anyone. With true freedom reigning in your mind and heart, you will soar like an eagle, far above every accusing voice, safe and secure in the arms of perfect love.

The Mind of Christ Rejoices in the Truth and Believes the Best of Every Person

1 Corinthians 13:6-8:

"Love does not pamper evil thoughts but nurtures the Word of God in the inner man. Love does not gloat over another man's sin but rejoices in the truth. Love never gives up, never loses faith, is always hopeful, and endures through every circumstance. It endures everything without weakening. Love is ever ready to believe the best of every person and is slow to expose. Love never fails" (paraphrase from various translations of the Bible).

The mind of perfect love does not pamper negative thoughts about anyone but rejoices in the truth about them. Jesus only said what He heard His Father say. So, what is the truth about you and your brothers and sisters in Christ? What does the Father and the Son think and feel toward us?

Listen to the voice of Truth:

We are the bride of Christ. In Song of Songs, Jesus looked at His bride in the middle of her greatest failure and said, *"My darling, everything about you is beautiful, and there is nothing at all wrong with you"* (Song of Songs 4:7, NCV).

Wow! What a beautiful picture of the mind of perfect love! Jesus has promised to never remember our sins

(Hebrews 8:12). He never focuses on our failures. He only reminds us who we are! He rejoices in the truth about us and sees the best in us even in the midst of our greatest failures. That's the mind of Christ—the mind of perfect love!

Since we have the mind of Christ, we don't focus on our failures nor do we focus on the failures of others. We see everyone, including ourselves, through the eyes of perfect love. When the negative thought comes to your mind that there is something wrong with you, you can boldly say, "Not today, devil! I have the mind of Christ! There is absolutely nothing wrong with me!"

One day, as I was sitting in my car, a negative thought came to my mind about a person who had done something wrong. This accusing, judgmental thought was trying to get me to focus on that person's failure and define them by their actions. I recognized that those thoughts were not my thoughts and that the devil was trying to corrupt my mind with lies. So, I replied, "Not today, devil! You are a liar! Those thoughts are not my thoughts!" I immediately invited the Holy Spirit to fill my mind with the truth and out of my heart came these words, "Father, I thank You that I have the mind of Christ toward this person. Thank You for changing the way I'm thinking toward them by the power of Your Spirit." I actually laughed at the devil as I realized how quickly his plan to bring destruction was squashed simply by embracing that I have the mind of Christ. Love rose up in my heart as I began to pray, "Father, I thank You that they have the mind of Christ. I trust You, Holy Spirit, to manifest that truth in their life." Freedom from negative, judgmental thoughts reigned in my mind. I experienced the fruit of perfect love—the thoughts, feelings and purposes of God's heart toward them by the power of God's Spirit.

We don't pamper negative thoughts about ourselves. We don't pamper negative thoughts about others because we have the mind of Christ. We hold the thoughts and the feelings and the purposes of His heart. We have a sound mind. We have a saved mind! Jesus rescued us from every negative, accusing, judgmental thought toward ourselves and toward others! He came to set our minds free with His perfect love!

Let me give you another example of how rejoicing in the truth has changed my life. I used to have such a negative opinion about my husband. All I could see were the things that he did wrong. I spent a lot of time thinking upon his faults and failures, and it was bringing destruction to our relationship. It was the enemy's plan, and I was oblivious to it. Negative, toxic thoughts were ruining my life and my marriage.

However, the day I asked Jesus to show me the truth that would set me free, the Holy Spirit began to renew my mind with the truth of our identity in Christ. I wept that day as the perfect love of the Father toward me overwhelmed my heart. I understood that day that even in the midst of all my failures, my good Father's opinion of me had never changed. He saw me as righteous, perfect, and approved in Christ. He saw me as beautiful and did not see one thing wrong with me! That was His mind toward me!

As the love of Christ healed my heart that day, the Holy Spirit filled my soul with such love for my husband, and the mind of Christ was manifested in my thoughts and feelings toward Him. I began to see Him through the eyes of perfect love.

No longer was I judging Him based on His actions and his failures, but I began to see what Jesus sees in Him. He was beautiful and there was nothing at all wrong with Him! He was a righteous, wonderful, and successful man in Christ. I was experiencing the mind of Christ toward him and peace flooded my soul. Embracing the truth saved my soul and my marriage!

I experienced the truth found in Romans 5:1-2, 5 that day:

"¹ Our faith in Jesus transfers God's righteousness to us and he now declares us flawless in his eyes. This means we can now enjoy true and lasting peace with God, all because of what our Lord Jesus, the Anointed One, has done for us. ² Our faith guarantees us permanent access into this marvelous kindness that has given us a perfect relationship with God. What incredible joy bursts forth within us as we keep on celebrating our hope of experiencing God's glory!

"⁵ And this hope is not a disappointing fantasy, because we can now experience the endless love of God cascading into our hearts through the Holy Spirit who lives in us!" (TPT).

One of the definitions of "God's glory" is "God's view and opinion" (blueletterbible.com). The glory of God is actually the very mind of Christ! What incredible joy bursts forth within us as we celebrate our hope of experiencing the mind of Christ in every area of our lives. When I understood the mind of Christ toward me and my husband was that we were flawless in His eyes, when I realized that He had given us His perfect righteousness as a gift of His grace, I experienced the endless love of God cascading into my heart through the Holy Spirit who lives in me.

The Spirit of God filled my thoughts with the mind of Christ toward my husband that day. Now that I understand that negative thoughts are not my thoughts, whenever I am tempted to think negatively about my husband, I invite the Holy Spirit to fill my mind with the truth and remind me who I am and who my husband is in Christ. One hundred percent of the time, when I am willing to let go of those negative thoughts, and I embrace the truth that I have the mind of Christ toward my husband, the Holy Spirit never fails to empower me to see him through the eyes of perfect love.

When I recognize those negative, toxic, destructive thoughts, I simply say, "Not today, devil! That thought is not my thought! I see the best in my husband because I have the mind of Christ!"

Could you imagine the effect this one truth could have on marriages and relationships? If husbands and wives owned the truth that the mind of Christ was their true identity, perfect love would reign in marriages. If brothers and sisters in Christ owned the truth that the mind of Christ is their true identity, perfect love would be the fruit of our lives toward each other. Instead of focusing on each other's faults, we would rejoice in the truth and see the best in each other. We would pray the mind of Christ over each other and see God's purpose for our lives manifest before our very eyes.

When you believe you have the mind of Christ—that you hold the thoughts, feelings and purposes of God's heart, you'll find your mind free from any negative thought about yourself or others! Because the mind of Christ believes the best about everyone!

When we see one of our brothers or sisters in Christ struggling in an area of their lives, instead of judging them and thinking negatively about them, our hearts are filled with love and compassion. We bear one another's burdens and so fulfill the law of love. We pray for one another and trust the Holy Spirit to manifest the mind of Christ in their thoughts. We never give up on them and we believe the best about them because we have the mind of Christ—the mind of perfect love!

Recently, I asked the Father, "When a person embraces the truth that they have the mind of perfect love, how will that affect their life? What will their life look like?" Immediately, He reminded me of Ephesians 3:17-20.

17 Then, by constantly using your faith, the life of Christ will be released deep inside you, and the resting place of his love will become the very source and root of your life.

18–19 Then you will be empowered to discover what every holy one experiences—the great magnitude of the astonishing love of Christ in all its dimensions. How deeply intimate and far-reaching is his love! How enduring and inclusive it is! Endless love beyond measurement that transcends our understanding—this extravagant love pours into you until you are filled to overflowing with the fullness of God!

20 Never doubt God's mighty power to work in you and accomplish all this. He will achieve infinitely more than your greatest request, your most unbelievable dream, and exceed your wildest imagination! He will outdo them all, for his miraculous power constantly energizes you" (TPT).

When you daily embrace the truth of your identity in Christ, the very life of Christ will be released deep inside you. His life is the mind of perfect love! It's a mind free from negative, toxic, accusing thoughts toward yourself and others. It's a mind that rejoices in the truth and believes the best about everyone. His extravagant love will pour into you until every thought is filled to overflowing with the fullness of God.

I love how this passage encourages us to never doubt God's mighty power to work in us and accomplish this. He will achieve infinitely more than your greatest request, your most unbelievable dreams, and exceed your wildest imaginations! He will outdo them all, for His miraculous resurrection power is at work in you when you embrace that you have the mind of Christ! Yes! You have the mind of perfect love! Embrace this truth about yourself today!

Reflection and Discussion Questions for Chapter 6

1. What truth did the Holy Spirit reveal to your heart today and how will you apply it in your life?

2. Describe the mind of perfect love according to 1 Corinthians 13:5. How will you respond when the enemy tries to corrupt your mind with an offense toward someone?

3. What was Jesus' thoughts and mind toward those who did Him wrong?

4. Read 1 Corinthians 13:6-8. What does this teach us about our true identity in Christ? How do you think it would affect marriages and relationships if every time a negative thought entered our mind toward someone, we embraced the truth that we have the mind of Christ?

5. What does it look like to believe the best about someone who is obviously making bad choices?

6. What does Ephesians 3:20 encourage us to do so that we can experience a life that exceeds our wildest imaginations and unbelievable dreams?

Chapter 7

The Mind of Christ is a Mind at Peace

1 Corinthians 2:16 says, *"...We have the mind of Christ (the Messiah) and do hold the thoughts (feelings and purposes) of His heart"* (AMPC).

Let's look at this same verse in The Passion Translation:

"For Who has ever intimately known the mind of the Lord Yahweh well enough to become his counselor? Christ has, and we possess Christ's perceptions."

What a different way to look at the mind of Christ. What does it mean to possess the perceptions of Christ?

Perception means a belief or opinion about something; the way we see or view a particular event or person. Your perception of something is the way that you think about it (Cambridge English Dictionary; Collins English Dictionary).

Our perception—how we see success, failure, physical death, friendships, love, and the world around us—is just a perception. Perception is our personal opinion, or our point of view, about any particular event. The truth about you is that you possess Christ's perceptions! You see things through His eyes. You hold His thoughts, feelings, and purposes toward yourself, toward others, and toward the situations that you face in life. That's your true identity concerning your thoughts and your mind.

The footnote of 1 Corinthians 2:16 from The Passion Translation gives us an even deeper understanding of what it means to have Christ's perceptions:

"That is, we believers possess the Holy Spirit, who reveals the thoughts and purposes of Christ. The revelation of the kingdom of God that Jesus preached was not understood by the intellect of men but by those who welcomed his truth. Humanly speaking, no one can understand the mysteries of God without the Holy Spirit. Those who have the Holy Spirit now possess the perceptions of Christ's mind and can implement his purposes on the earth" (https://www.biblegateway.com/passage/?search=1+Cor+2%3A16&version=TPT).

When we own that we have the mind of Christ, we have His perceptions about everything. Everywhere we go, we will see the world through His view and opinion. Everything we say and everything we do will bring forth God's kingdom in the earth. Just like Jesus, we will only say what we hear our Father say and only do what we see our Father do, and we will see His glory manifest all around us!

If the mind of Christ is our true identity, that means we possess Christ's belief or opinion about everything. Since we possess Christ's perceptions, we see people through our Father's eyes. His opinion of you and others is your opinion. When we own our true identity when it comes to our minds and our thoughts, we invite Him to change the way we see everything.

I often find myself praying, "Father, I have the mind of Christ. I thank You that I see this situation or this person through Your eyes." As we invite the Holy Spirit to change the way we see and think, we will experience peace in every situation because Jesus is the Prince of Peace, and everything He thinks produces peace.

I love thinking on the truth that I am one with the Prince of Peace. Fearful, anxious, and stress-filled thoughts are not the mind of Christ, so they are not a part of our minds either. We won't tolerate them when we own our true identity. Jesus has a righteous mind and so do you. That means you think right in every situation. That is a powerful truth to believe about yourself. I've recently found myself thinking, "I have a righteous mind. I think right about myself. I think right about others. I think right about every situation because I have a righteous mind. I have the mind of Christ. That's what true about me!"

If a feeling of worry or concern comes up in my heart, I simply turn my thoughts to Jesus and say, "Jesus, I am one with You. I have Your mind. I possess Your view and opinion about this situation, and You are at perfect peace about it." When we begin to commune with Jesus that way and focus on the truth that we are one with Him, the Spirit of God brings to our thoughts and minds the perceptions of Christ.

That's the Holy Spirit's job. Isn't that a beautiful thing to know? It's not your job to try to think right. It's not your job to try to see things through God's eyes, but rather to trust the Holy Spirit to change your perception in every situation. Imagine living your life with the perceptions of Christ. You would live in perfect and constant peace. It's as simple as owning that you have the mind of Christ and trusting Him to manifest His glory (His view and opinion) in your thoughts and mind. What a light and easy way to live!

In John 14:27 Jesus said, *"I am leaving you with a gift— peace of mind and heart. And the peace I give is a gift the world cannot give. So don't be troubled or afraid"* (NLT).

Peace means "a state free of oppressive and unpleasant thoughts and emotions; the absence of mental stress or anxiety" (https://www.definitions.net/definition/peace).

This is the peace that Jesus gave you—a mind free of oppressive and unpleasant thoughts and emotions; a mind absent of mental stress or anxiety. Jesus gave you the gift of peace of mind.

The Mind of Christ Is a Mind at Peace with Yourself

You possess Christ's perceptions of you! You have your Father's view and opinion about yourself!

Romans 5:1:

"Our faith in Jesus transfers God's righteousness to us and he now declares us flawless in his eyes. This means we can now enjoy true and lasting peace with God, all because of what our Lord Jesus, the Anointed One, has done for us" (TPT).

We enjoy true and lasting peace of mind when we see ourselves through our Father's eyes. He sees us as righteous and flawless in Christ. We have a righteous mind because of what Jesus did for us. When we own our true identity about our thoughts and our minds, we experience a mind at peace.

My friend, Liza, is a living testimony of this truth. Listen to her powerful testimony:

"As long as I can remember, I struggled with depression and negative thoughts about myself. I have been a Christian my whole life, but I'd been in dark places for years. Those days were so hard! The struggle was real! Negative thoughts could be so overwhelming that I condemned myself over thinking those thoughts. This kept me away from running to Jesus so He could set me free. The first time I heard Connie teach about the mind of Christ, I thought, *WOW! That sounds amazing! I need to get this! I need to understand how to do that! How do I believe that I have the mind of Christ?*

"At the Tulsa conference in October 2018, Connie taught, 'The struggle is over! You HAVE the mind of Christ!' and it hit me right in my heart! I learned that the truth that sets me free is always a revelation of my true identity in Christ. I have the mind of Christ. Negative thoughts are not my thoughts. When you embrace the truth of Jesus over yourself, the negative thoughts will leave. The mind of Christ is never negative. It is a mind of love and peace! WOW!

"A few days later, we had Bible study, and while my friends were talking, I had my own talk with Jesus. I was telling Him, *I think I'm really getting this, Jesus.* He whispered in my heart, 'You have the mind of Christ, My Liza. Don't try to get it, just own it!' WOW! I said, *Yes, Jesus, I will!* And I embraced the mind of Christ! I own it! It is mine because I am one with my Jesus!

"What happened when I embraced and owned the mind of Christ is amazing! Just thinking of it makes me want to do a happy dance! My thoughts are free! My head feels so light! For the first time in my life, I know how it feels to have a sound mind! I have so much more peace and joy in my heart and mind than ever before.

"And, yes, negative thoughts try to come in, but I have the power to say, 'No! They are not my thoughts! I have the mind of Christ!' The struggle really is over! I am so thankful! He turned my mourning into dancing, my sorrow into joy. Jesus has set me free from depression and negative thoughts! My mind is now full of peace and joy! Thank You, Jesus!"

Liza is a living testimony of the power of owning the mind of Christ. As she embraced her true identity, the Spirit of God empowered her to see herself through the Father's eyes. She experienced the mind of Christ—a mind at peace with herself.

Her testimony reminds me of God's promise in Isaiah 54:14 and 17:

"¹⁴ You will be firmly established in righteousness: You will be far from [even the thought of] oppression, for you will not fear, And from terror, for it will not come near you" (AMP).

"¹⁷ ...No weapon turned against you will succeed. You will silence every voice raised up to accuse you. These benefits are enjoyed by the servants of the LORD; their vindication will come from me. I, the LORD, have spoken!" (NLT).

As Liza's heart became firmly established in her righteous identity in Christ, the thoughts of oppression stayed far from her. She silenced every negative, accusing thought that the enemy brought to her mind by saying, "No! That's not my thought, and that's not true about me! I have the mind of Christ!" The enemy's plan to oppress her did not succeed anymore because she owned the truth that she had the mind of Christ!

The Mind of Christ is a Mind at Peace About Others

You possess Christ's perceptions of others! You have your Father's view and opinion of them.

Ephesians 2:14-18 says, *"Our reconciling "Peace" is Jesus! He has made Jew and non-Jew one in Christ. By dying as our sacrifice, he has broken down every wall of prejudice that separated us and has now made us equal through our union with Christ. Ethnic hatred has been dissolved by the crucifixion of his precious body on the cross. The legal code* that stood condemning every one of us has now been repealed by his command. *His triune essence has made peace between us by starting over—forming one new race of humanity, Jews and non-Jews fused together!*

"Two have now become one, and we live restored to God and reconciled in the body of Christ. Through his crucifixion, hatred died. For the Messiah has come to preach this sweet message of peace to you, the ones who were distant, and to those who are near. And now, because we are united to Christ, we both have equal and direct access in the realm of the Holy Spirit to come before the Father!" (TPT).

Did you hear that truth? Ethnic hatred has died. It was dissolved in the crucifixion of Jesus. Jesus died for all mankind. He proved that everyone was of equal value. He proved that no man is better or worse than another. His death, burial, and resurrection proved how He felt about mankind. He made us one in value, one in His love. He doesn't love me anymore than He loves the one who has rejected Him.

When we have Christ's perceptions, we see people as equal. We see our brothers and sisters as equal with us, not inferior or superior. We no longer see them in the flesh, but we see them in the spirit because we possess Christ's perceptions.

2 Corinthians 5:16-17:

"So then, from now on, we have a new perspective that refuses to evaluate people merely by their outward appearances. For that's how we once viewed the Anointed One, but no longer do we see him with limited human insight.

Now, if anyone is enfolded into Christ, he has become an entirely new creation. All that is related to the old order has vanished. Behold, everything is fresh and new" (TPT).

The Power of Praying the Mind of Christ Over Those You Love

2 Corinthians 5:16-17 says that we no longer view people by their outward appearance or identify them with the flesh. We define them by their new creation in Christ Jesus. When we see our brothers or sisters in Christ struggling, we don't judge them, we declare the truth about them and trust the Holy Spirit to manifest it in their lives. One of the most powerful truths we can pray and declare is that they have the mind of Christ.

I want to share with you one of the most amazing miracles of deliverance that I have ever witnessed in my entire life. My good friends, Larry and Heather Baeumel, who pastor True Grace Church in Redlands, CA, have a 34-year-old daughter named Audrey. She had been homeless and addicted to meth for 18 years. They had been praying for her for a long time.

On Sunday, I preached the message on the mind of Christ and how we are one with Jesus and have been given His mind. I shared my own testimony about my daughter, Victoria, and how praying the mind of Christ over her brought about the manifestation of God's glory in her life.

After that Sunday service, Larry and Heather came to me and said, "We have been praying for Audrey for a long time, but we got a revelation of her being one with Jesus and having His mind this weekend that has changed the way we see her and the way we pray for her. She does not have an addicted mind. She has the mind of Christ! That is what is true about her, no matter where she lives, what she's doing, or what the circumstances may be."

We all began to rejoice in the truth about Audrey and began to pray in agreement and declare that she was one with Jesus and had the mind of Christ!

I remember declaring, "Audrey, come home!" It was a powerful time of prayer!

On Monday, we decided to drive to the beach. While we were there, the most amazing thing happened. Heather got a phone call from Audrey. Audrey told her that she had been sleeping for a day and a half in a hole under the bridge where she and her boyfriend, Fernando, lived with their two puppy dogs.

She had awakened to go get something to eat and when she returned, fire was bursting out of the entrance to where she lived. The propane tanks they used to keep warm and make food had exploded, and liquid fire was coming out of the entrance. Her puppies were still inside and she ran to save them, but it was too late.

Her boyfriend grabbed her and said, "Audrey, the puppies are gone! There is no way they can survive." But Audrey began to cry out, "NO, Jesus will save our puppies! Jesus will save our puppies!" She had to wait until the fire died down; it had been burning and smoldering for over ten hours.

When she was finally able to enter the hole, she heard a sound that brought joy to her heart. Her puppies were whimpering inside this hole that had been an inferno just hours before. Jesus had indeed saved her puppies, and she was crying on the phone, telling her mom, "Jesus, saved my puppies! He loves me, Mom! Jesus saved my puppies! I'm done living here. I don't want to live this way anymore! I want to come home!"

That day, the mind of Christ was manifested in Audrey's thoughts, and Jesus performed a miracle to prove His love for her. As a result, after being homeless for 18 years, Audrey came home in her right mind!

Within three months, Audrey and Fernando were completely off of drugs. They both testified to the love of their good Father and how Jesus rescued them! Audrey and Fernando both began to declare to each other that they have the mind of Christ. They both got jobs and were married on June 30, 2019. They began to minister to the homeless people they had lived with for so long! Talk about a glorious deliverance!

Just as Isaiah 61:4 promises, Jesus literally turned their ashes into beauty, their sorrow into joy, and their despair into songs of praise. He established their hearts in the truth that they are one with Jesus and they have His mind. And Heather and Larry saw the glory of God manifest in their daughter's life!

Wow! We witnessed the power of embracing that we are one with Jesus and that we hold His thoughts, feelings and the purposes of His heart toward others. We have the mind of perfect love toward those who are caught in sin, and we watched our good Father manifest His good purpose for Audrey's life right before our eyes. That's the power of embracing that we have the mind of Christ—the mind of perfect peace!

The Mind of Christ Is a Mind at Peace and Every Negative Circumstance

You possess Christ's perceptions about every situation in your life. You have your Father's view and opinion. When we own the mind of Christ, we begin to see from Christ's perspective. We see our circumstances through Christ's eyes and we enjoy true and lasting peace.

John 16:33:

"I have told you these things, so that in Me you may have [perfect] peace and confidence. In the world you have tribulation and trials and distress and frustration; but be of good cheer [take courage; be confident, certain,

*undaunted]! For I have overcome the world. [I have
deprived it of power to harm you and have conquered it
for you.]"* (AMPC).

Christ's perception of every trial you go through in this
life is seen very clearly in this verse. Jesus said, "I'm giving
you My perception so that you might have perfect peace and
confidence. In this world, you will have trials, temptations,
distress, and frustrations, but be of good cheer; I have
overcome the world! I have risen from the dead! I have
conquered sin and death."

Jesus conquered everything associated with sin and
death in His death burial and resurrection and made us one
with Him! He did this so we can look at every circumstance
of our lives with the perspective that, "We win! We've been
made righteous in Jesus, and all the promises of God are
'Yes!' and 'Amen!' in our lives! We are more than
conquerors through Him who loves us! The story has already
been written and Jesus is the final word over our lives and
the lives of those we love!"

I experienced a negative circumstance when one of my
sons made a really bad decision and got himself thrown into
jail. Talk about a trial and temptation for this momma's
heart. I remember laying on my bed, crying. I was so upset
and felt like God had failed me. I definitely wasn't
experiencing the mind of Christ in that moment. I was taking
on my own opinion of the situation.

Then I turned my thoughts to Jesus and said, "Jesus, help
me! I'm not seeing this through Your eyes. Help me, Holy
Spirit, to see the truth that will set me free!" I remember the
sweet sound of correction coming to my heart. I heard Jesus
speak to my heart, "Connie, this does not change who your
son is, and it does not change what I have promised
concerning him. I am working every detail of his life into
something good."

At first my thoughts were filled with discouragement, sadness, doubt, and frustration, but as the Holy Spirit changed my perspective, peace like a river flooded my soul and I began to experience the mind of Christ about the situation.

I remember my daughter-in-law, Jessica, called me in the middle of that trial to remind me of John 16:33. She said, "Connie, Jesus said in this world we'd have trials and temptations, but He has already conquered the world for us. You are already victorious in Jesus!"

What a perspective! What peace we have in Jesus! I remember rejoicing as my heart began to embrace the truth that even this was going to work out for my son's good! I watched Jesus redeem the situation and bring my son out even stronger in his faith than he was before. I experienced peace and confidence in the middle of that trial, and I watched the glory of God manifest in my son's life because I have the mind of Christ—and so does he!

Philippians 4:6-9 says, *"Don't fret or worry. Instead of worrying, pray. Let petitions and praises shape your worries into prayers, letting God know your concerns. Before you know it, a sense of God's wholeness, everything coming together for good, will come and settle you down. It's wonderful what happens when Christ displaces worry at the center of your life.*

Summing it all up, friends, I'd say you'll do best by filling your minds and meditating on things true, noble, reputable, authentic, compelling, gracious—the best, not the worst; the beautiful, not the ugly; things to praise, not things to curse. Put into practice what you learned from me, what you heard and saw and realized. Do that, and God, who makes everything work together, will work you into his most excellent harmonies" (MSG).

Isaiah 26:3 says, *"You will keep in perfect peace all who trust in you, all whose thoughts are fixed on you!"* (NLT).

Remember, you have the mind of Christ! You have a mind that is at peace with yourself, a mind that is at peace with others, and a mind that is at peace in every situation you encounter in life. You have His perspective about everything! You have a righteous mind! You think right in every situation! Own the truth about your mind and your thoughts, and watch God's glory (His view and opinion) manifest in every area of your life!

Reflection and Discussion Questions for Chapter 7

1. What is the main truth that spoke to you in this chapter and how will you apply it to your life?

2. What is a perception? What does it mean to have Christ's perceptions?

3. Why can you enjoy true and lasting peace with God? (Romans 5:1).

4. Have you ever felt depressed? Have you ever struggled with fearful thoughts? What did you learn from Liza's testimony about the power of embracing your true identity about your mind?

5. How did Audrey's story touch your heart? Do you have a child or someone you love who is caught in addiction or struggling in their minds? How can praying the mind of Christ over them change their lives?

6. What is the mind of Christ toward every trial or temptation that comes at you in this world? (John 16:33).

Take time to pray over any situation that may be concerning your heart today! Remember, you have the mind of Christ! You hold the thoughts, feelings, and purposes of God's heart, so watch His glory manifest in your life and in the lives of those you love!

Chapter 8

Give Your Carnal Mind a Decent Burial!

Something amazing happened to your mind in the resurrection of Jesus Christ. When you were born again, the same Spirit that raised Jesus from the dead came to live in you to manifest the mind of Christ in your thoughts, feelings, and the purposes of your heart.

Your old identity was crucified with Jesus. Your old anxious, fearful, depressed, guilty, condemned, sinful nature died with Jesus, and you were resurrected with Him with a brand-new righteous nature and a brand-new mind! You were given the very mind of Christ! In this chapter, we're going to give our old carnal nature a decent burial, own the mind of Christ as our true identity once and for all, and get on living the glorious life that our Jesus came to give us!

Do you have two natures? Do you have two minds? Sounds crazy doesn't it? But that's what I used to believe! That's why I used to struggle all the time with doubt, worry, fear, guilt, comparison, and jealousy. That is the fruit of a person's life who lives double minded and doesn't embrace the truth about who they truly are in Jesus!

James 1:8 says, *"[For being as he is] a man of two minds (hesitating, dubious, irresolute), [he is] unstable and unreliable and uncertain about everything [he thinks, feels, decides]"* (AMPC).

But the struggle in our minds is over when we embrace the truth that we have one nature and one mind! You are the righteousness of God in Christ Jesus, and you have a righteous mind—the very mind of Christ! When you embrace the truth about your righteous identity in Jesus, you'll live stable and confident about everything you think, feel, and decide!

Isaiah 32:17 says, *"And the effect of righteousness will be peace [internal and external], and the result of righteousness will be quietness and confident trust forever"* (AMPC).

What About the Carnal Mind?

Even though 1 Corinthians 2:16 teaches us that we have the mind of Christ, for many years of my Christian life I was taught and believed that I also had a carnal mind. When we hold onto these two opposing beliefs about our identity, it keeps us in a constant struggle with condemnation, anxiety, worry, fear, stress, confusion, and trying to fix our minds with our own human effort.

The truth is you do not have a dual nature or a dual identity. Ask yourself this question, "Do I have a carnal mind? Or do I have the mind of Christ?" Because only one of those terms defines the truth about your mind, and the identity you embrace will determine the fruit of your life. The Apostle Paul explains in 1 Corinthians 3:1-3 that when we don't embrace the truth that we have the mind of Christ, we live our lives acting like unbelievers.

Let's look at 1 Corinthians chapters 2 and 3 to get the full context of the truth that the Apostle Paul was teaching

us concerning the mind of Christ. In 1 Corinthians 2:2, the Apostle Paul begins by saying, *"For I determined not to know anything among you except Jesus Christ and Him crucified"* (NKJV). He then goes on to explain in great detail in 1 Corinthians 2:3-16 how the death, burial, and resurrection of Jesus brought us into His glory and gave us the very mind of Christ. He ends this chapter with 1 Corinthians 2:16, which reveals this powerful truth about our identity in Jesus: *"We have the mind of Christ."*

In the very next verse, beginning in 1 Corinthians 3, the Apostle Paul begins to correct wrong behavior that was coming from Christians who did not fully understand what happened in the death, burial, and resurrection of Jesus and, therefore, were not believing the truth that he taught in 1 Corinthians 2 about their new identity concerning their minds.

In 1 Corinthians 3:1-3 he says, *"And I, brethren, could not speak to you as to spiritual people but as to **carnal**, as to babes in Christ. I fed you with milk and not with solid food; for until now **you were not able to receive it**, and even now you are still not able; for you are still **carnal**. For where there are envy, strife, and divisions among you, are you not **carnal** and behaving like mere men?"* (NKJV, emphasis added).

In The Passion Translation, 1 Corinthians 3:3 and 16 read, *"³ For you are living your lives dominated by the mind-set of the flesh. Ask yourselves: Is there jealousy among you? Do you compare yourselves with others? Do you quarrel like children and end up taking sides? If so, this proves that you are living your lives centered on yourselves, dominated by the mind-set of the flesh, and behaving like unbelievers.*

¹⁶ Don't you realize that together you have become God's inner sanctuary and that the Spirit of God makes his permanent home in you?"

Wow! The Apostle Paul was showing us the fruit of the life of a Christian who will not receive the truth that they have the mind of Christ. Right after he said, "We have the mind of Christ," he described carnal people as those who would not receive this truth. He explained that if the fruit of our lives is jealousy, comparing ourselves to each other, strife, envy and division among us, then we are behaving like those who don't believe they have the mind of Christ. We are behaving as those who don't believe in the death, burial, and resurrection of Jesus. We are still identifying with our old identity instead of identifying with Jesus and our new righteous identity in Him.

But just like a good Father, in 1 Corinthians 3:16, he reminds us again who we truly are in Christ. He says, "Remember, who you are! You are the temple of God and the Spirit of God dwells in you." In other words, "Remember, you are of the Spirit, and you have the mind of Christ! For when we rely on the Holy Spirit within us and believe the truth that we have the mind of Christ, the Spirit of God manifests that truth in our lives."

So, let's ask ourselves this question again: "Do I have a carnal mind? Or do I have the mind of Christ?" Because the identity you embrace will determine the fruit of your life.

The Meaning of the Word "Carnal"

"Carnal" comes from the Greek word *sarkikos* (Strong's G4559) and it means "having the nature of flesh; governed by mere human nature not by the Spirit of God" (blueletterbible.com).

The word "carnal" actually describes our old nature of the flesh that died with Jesus. It literally means one who is governed by their human nature and not by the Spirit of God.

The Bible teaches us that our old carnal nature ruled by the flesh died with Jesus, and our old guilty, condemned carnal mind was buried with Him too.

Colossians 2:11-12 says, *"In him you were also circumcised with a circumcision not performed by human hands. Your whole self ruled by the flesh was put off when you were circumcised by Christ, having been buried with him in baptism, in which you were also raised with him through your faith in the working of God, who raised him from the dead"* (NIV).

The word "flesh" in this Scripture comes from the Greek word *sarx,* and it actually means "carnally minded; the flesh, denotes mere human nature, the earthly nature of man apart from divine influence, and therefore prone to sin and opposed to God" (Strong's G4561; blueletterbible.com).

When I saw that the word "flesh"—that describes our old nature that was cut off from us when we died with Jesus— actually meant carnally minded, my spirit jumped within me! For the first time, I fully understood that our carnal mind, which was part of our carnal nature, was also cut away from us when we were crucified with Jesus. Our carnal mind died with Jesus!

The only reason we think and act badly as a new creation in Christ is because we either don't know or have forgotten who we really are in Him. That's why there was jealousy, comparison and division among the Corinthians, and the Apostle Paul said, "You are acting like mere men. You are acting like unbelievers. Don't you understand who you really are?"

According to the definition of *sarx,* our flesh is our earthly nature that was apart from divine influence, was prone to sin, opposed to God, and carnally minded. With this in mind, if it's true that your whole self that was ruled by the flesh died with Jesus, then that means your carnal mind died with Jesus too! When you believed in His resurrection, you were raised with Him with a brand-new nature and a brand-new mind.

Let's read Colossians 2:11-15 in The Passion Translation:

"Through our union with him we have experienced circumcision of heart. All of the guilt and power of sin has been cut away and is now extinct because of what Christ, the Anointed One, has accomplished for us. For we've been buried with him into his death. Our "baptism into death" also means we were raised with him when we believed in God's resurrection power, the power that raised him from death's realm. This "realm of death" describes our former state, for we were held in sin's grasp. But now, we've been resurrected out of that "realm of death" never to return, for we are forever alive and forgiven of all our sins! He canceled out every legal violation we had on our record and the old arrest warrant that stood to indict us. He erased it all—our sins, our stained soul—he deleted it all and they cannot be retrieved! Everything we once were in Adam has been placed onto his cross and nailed permanently there as a public display of cancellation. Then Jesus made a public spectacle of all the powers and principalities of darkness, stripping away from them every weapon and all their spiritual authority and power to accuse us. And by the power of the cross, Jesus led them around as prisoners in a procession of triumph. He was not their prisoner; they were his!" (TPT).

Isn't this the best news you've ever heard! Through your union with Jesus, your old carnal man of the flesh, and it's guilt-ridden mind, was cut away from you and made extinct. Extinct means "died out, dead, no longer existing, destroyed, exterminated" (dictionary.com).

When you believed in the power that raised Jesus from the dead, everything associated with your carnal man of the flesh—your fearful, worried, guilt-ridden, condemned, shameful, anxious, and depressed mind—died and was exterminated when it was buried with Jesus. And you were raised with Him with a brand-new nature, with a brand-new mind, filled with His love, joy, peace, faith, confidence, and security. He erased your stained soul. He erased your stained mind, will, and emotions and gave you a brand-new heart and a brand-new mind.

Everything you were in Adam has been placed onto His cross and has stayed permanently dead. Then Jesus stripped the enemy of all his power to accuse you. He led the enemy around as His prisoner in a procession of triumph.

Romans 8:1 tells us, *"The case is closed! There is no more accusing voice of condemnation against those who live in life-union with Jesus!"* (TPT).

Hebrews 10:1-23 teaches that the blood of Jesus cleansed your mind from a guilty conscience! That's what's true about your mind, and you don't have to put up with the devil accusing you one more moment in your life! Jesus freed your mind from all guilt in His resurrection, and you experience that freedom when you believe it!

Romans 8:1 says, *"With the arrival of Jesus, the Messiah, that fateful dilemma is resolved. Those who enter into Christ's being-here-for-us no longer have to live under a continuous, low-lying black cloud. A new power is in operation. The Spirit of life in Christ, like a strong wind, has magnificently cleared the air, freeing you from a fated lifetime of brutal tyranny at the hands of sin and death"* (MSG).

How do you enter into Christ being here for you and no longer live under a continuous, low-lying dark cloud of anxiety, depression, condemnation and shame? How can you live free from a condemned and guilty mind?

2 Corinthians 10:4-5 says, *"(For the weapons of our warfare are not carnal, but mighty through God to the pulling down of strong holds;) Casting down imaginations, and every high thing that exalteth itself against the knowledge of God, and bringing into captivity every thought to the obedience of Christ"* (KJV).

In The Passion Translation, 2 Corinthians 10:5 says, *"...We capture, like prisoners of war, every thought and insist that it bow in obedience to the Anointed One."*

Remember, those guilty, accusing, negative thoughts are not your thoughts! So you can tell them, "NO! Access denied! No negative thoughts allowed! I am one with Jesus! I have the mind of Christ!"

Don't let the devil lie to you and tell you that you have any other mind than the mind of Christ. Cast down every thought that doesn't belong to you and make it bow to the resurrection power of Jesus! Capture those accusing, negative thoughts like prisoners of war and make them bow in obedience to Jesus! They must go because they don't belong to you anymore. You have a brand-new mind. You can live free from all anxiety, worry, fear, guilt, or shame because of what Jesus has accomplished for you!

There is a struggle that continues to go on in the mind of God's children when they believe they have a carnal nature and a righteous nature. The Apostle Paul describes the struggle of one who holds onto the idea that they have two natures and two minds. When we believe we have two identities, the struggle in our minds continues.

The Apostle Paul describes this struggle in Romans 7:21-25:

"21 I have discovered this principle of life—that when I want to do what is right, I inevitably do what is wrong. 22 I love God's law with all my heart. 23 But there is

another power within me that is at war with my mind. This power makes me a slave to the sin that is still within me. 24 Oh, what a miserable person I am! Who will free me from this life that is dominated by sin and death? 25 Thank God! The answer is in Jesus Christ our Lord. So you see how it is: In my mind I really want to obey God's law, but because of my sinful nature I am a slave to sin" (NLT).

Can you see the struggle in the mind in these verses? The Apostle Paul is describing the life of a person who is holding onto two identities. There is a power within them that is at war with their minds that makes them a slave to sin. When a person holds onto the idea that they still have a carnal nature or a carnal mind, they constantly struggle with worry, fear, comparison, jealousy, guilt and condemnation. The struggle is real! In verse 24, the Apostle Paul says, "Oh, what a miserable person I am! Who will free me from this constant battle in my mind?"

Oh, how I can relate to this battle in the mind! I used to feel this way all the time. I would actually read this passage of Scripture and think, *That's exactly how I feel! What an unhappy person I am!* I stopped at verse 24 and lived there for many years of my Christian life. How sad! When the answer to my freedom was in the very next verse!

In verse 25 the Apostle Paul gives the answer to this constant struggle in the mind: *"Thank God! The answer is in Jesus Christ our Lord!"* When we embrace our true identity in Christ, the struggle ends, and we experience freedom in our minds.

In the very next verse, in Romans 8:1, the Apostle Paul describes this freedom: *"So now the case is closed! There remains no more accusing voice of condemnation against those who are joined in life-union with Jesus"*! (TPT). When you live in life-union with Jesus, you own the mind of Christ, and those negative, condemning voices lose their power in your life!

Read Romans 8:5-9:

"For those who live according to the flesh set their minds on the things of the flesh, but those who live according to the Spirit, the things of the Spirit. For to be carnally minded is death, but to be spiritually minded is life and peace. Because the carnal mind is enmity against God; for it is not subject to the law of God, nor indeed can be. So then, those who are in the flesh cannot please God. But you are not in the flesh but in the Spirit, if indeed the Spirit of God dwells in you" (NKJV).

Verse 5 says that when you identify with the flesh, you set your mind on the natural man. You define yourself "in the flesh" rather than "in the spirit." Verse 6 says to be carnally minded is death.

The word "death" in this verse comes from the Greek word *thanatos* (Strong's G2288) and it means "separated from the life of God; a conscious existence of separation from God; death is the opposite of life thus life is a conscious existence of union with God" (See Vine's Expository Dictionary Entry at https://www.blueletterbible.org/lang/lexicon/lexicon.cfm?Strongs=G2288&t=NKJV).

Since death is a conscious existence of separation from Jesus, to be carnally minded means to see yourself as separated from Him. One who believes they still have a carnal nature and a carnal mind identifies with their flesh and struggles with worry, fear, condemnation, shame, guilt, jealousy, comparison, and all kinds of dead works in their life (Galatians 5:19-21).

But when you identify with the Spirit, you set your mind on Jesus and your union with Him. Verse 6 says to be spiritually minded brings life and peace. Since life is a conscious existence of union with God, to be spiritually minded is to see yourself as a brand-new creation in Jesus. When you see yourself as one with Jesus, you believe you have His mind, and the Holy Spirit brings forth the fruit of the Spirit in your life (Galatians 5:22-25).

For many years of my Christian life, I heard it taught that we have a carnal mind. I have come to understand through the Scriptures that is not true about my new nature in Jesus. But just the other day, as I was thinking upon this teaching, I went back to Romans 8:7 and read what it means to have a carnal mind.

Verse 7 says that the carnal mind is at enmity with God. What does it mean to be at enmity with God? Enmity means "the state or feeling of being actively opposed or hostile to someone or something. Synomyns: hostility, animosity, opposition, dissention, bitterness, resentment, dislike, hatred, loathing" (https://www.lexico.com/en/ definition/enmity).

When I realized that to believe I have a carnal mind meant that I have a mind that is actively opposed and hostile to God, it became very clear why the enemy has deceived so many of God's children into embracing this identity about their minds. A carnal mind has animosity, dissention, bitterness, resentment, dislike and even hatred for God.

WOW! Isn't that what the enemy wants? For us to be opposed to our good Father? I will never believe I have a carnal mind because that's not who I am. I love my good Father with all my heart, with all my mind, and with all my soul! That's what is true about me, and that's what is true about you! Because we have the mind of Christ!

In verse 9, the Apostle Paul makes this truth about our identity very clear when He says, "**But you are not in the flesh** (that's not who you are anymore)." He says that if the Spirit of God dwells in you, then you are in the Spirit. You are one with Jesus, and you have His mind.

It's Time to Give Your Carnal Mind a Decent Burial and Get on With Your New Life!

Now, let's read Romans 8:10-17:

"¹⁰ It stands to reason, doesn't it, that if the alive-and-present God who raised Jesus from the dead moves into your life, he'll do the same thing in you that he did in Jesus, bringing you alive to himself? ¹¹ When God lives and breathes in you (and he does, as surely as he did in Jesus), you are delivered from that dead life. With his Spirit living in you, your body will be as alive as Christ's! ¹²⁻¹⁴ So don't you see that we don't owe this old do-it-yourself life one red cent. There's nothing in it for us, nothing at all. The best thing to do is give it a decent burial and get on with your new life. God's Spirit beckons. There are things to do and places to go!

¹⁵⁻¹⁷ This resurrection life you received from God is not a timid, grave-tending life. It's adventurously expectant, greeting God with a childlike "What's next, Papa?" God's Spirit touches our spirits and confirms who we really are. We know who he is, and we know who we are: Father and children. And we know we are going to get what's coming to us—an unbelievable inheritance!" (MSG).

The struggle is over! Your carnal nature and your carnal mind died with Jesus. That confused, depressed, addicted, guilty, stressed-out, anxious mind, that compares itself with everyone else, died with Jesus and it's time to give it a decent burial. You have a brand-new life to live!

The same power that raised Jesus from the dead lives in you to bring life to your thoughts and your mind. You were resurrected with the very mind of Christ! This resurrection life you received is not a grave-tending life. You don't owe that do-it-yourself-life one red cent! There is nothing in it for you but a continual struggle with addiction, fear, worry, guilt and condemnation.

Now you can live adventurously expectant with a childlike, "What's next, Papa?" God's spirit touches your spirit and confirms that you are His beloved child and your inheritance is the mind of Christ! You've been resurrected with the very life of Christ!

We see this truth again in Romans 6:6-11:

"6 For we know that our old self was crucified with him so that the body ruled by sin might be done away with, that we should no longer be slaves to sin— 7 because anyone who has died has been set free from sin.

8 Now if we died with Christ, we believe that we will also live with him. 9 For we know that since Christ was raised from the dead, he cannot die again; death no longer has mastery over him. 10 The death he died, he died to sin once for all; but the life he lives, he lives to God.

11 In the same way, count yourselves dead to sin but alive to God in Christ Jesus" (NIV).

Could it be any clearer? Verse 6 tells us our old self was crucified with Jesus so that our old carnal nature and it's carnal mind that was ruled by sin might be done away with, so that we would no longer be slaves to sin. Just as Jesus died to sin once and for all and rose to life again, consider yourself also dead to sin but alive in Christ Jesus!

Romans 6:11 says, *"So let it be the same way with you! Since you are now joined with him, you must continually view yourselves as dead and unresponsive to sin's appeal while living daily for God's pleasure in union with Jesus, the Anointed One"* (TPT).

What Does It Mean to View Yourself as Dead to Sin and Alive in Christ?

Let me give you an example from my own life. I shared in a previous chapter how I used to struggle with jealousy and often compared myself to others. The reason I did so is because I viewed myself in the flesh. I believed the lie that I was not as blessed as other Christians. I believed I lacked in some way. I thought I wasn't as favored or as good as them. I was identifying with my dead carnal nature and it was producing dead works in my life.

But when I understood that my carnal nature was dead, and that I now had a new righteous identity in Jesus, I began viewing myself as dead to jealousy. When jealous thoughts tried to enter my mind, I would say, "That's not who I am! I am dead to that! I am blessed and favored because of Jesus!" That's when jealousy lost its power in my life. That's when I experienced true freedom in my mind!

This is how important it is to consider your carnal nature dead and to see yourself as a brand-new creation in Christ Jesus with a brand-new mind! Your complete freedom depends on it! So, the next time a negative thought or temptation comes to your mind, consider your carnal nature dead and say, "No, that's not my thought! That's not who I am! I am the righteousness of God in Christ, and I have a righteous mind!" When you give your carnal mind a decent burial and you embrace the truth that you've been resurrected with the mind of Christ, you'll experience true freedom in your mind! The struggle is over! You've been resurrected to a brand-new life!

Galatians 2:20 says, *"My old identity has been co-crucified with Messiah and no longer lives; for the nails of his cross crucified me with him. And now the essence of this new life is no longer mine, for the Anointed One lives his life through me—we live in union as one! My new life is empowered by the faith of the Son of God who loves me so much that he gave himself for me, and dispenses his life into mine!"* (TPT).

Reflection and Discussion Questions for Chapter 8

1. What is the main truth that spoke to you in this chapter and how will you apply it to your life?

2. What did James 1:8 reveal about a person who holds onto two minds?

3. How does a person behave who does not receive the truth that they have the mind of Christ? (1 Corinthians 3:3).

4. Do you have the mind of Christ or do you have a carnal mind? Which of these defines your identity in Christ?

5. What happened to your carnal nature and your carnal mind in the death, burial and resurrection of Jesus? (Colossians 2:11-15).

6. If you are struggling in your mind, what is the answer? (Romans 7:21-25).

7. What does it mean to be carnally minded versus spiritually minded, and what does each produce in our lives? (Romans 8:5-9). What truth about your true identity did the Apostle Paul teach us in verse 9?

8. How do we give our carnal mind a decent burial and get on living the glorious life Jesus came to give us? (Romans 8:10-17).

9. Read Galatians 2:20 again. What powerful truth is revealed in this verse, and how can you apply it in your life?

The Mind of Christ
is the
Promises of God

In this book, you've learned a lot about what it means to have the mind of Christ. I would like to end this book with this section that lists the promises you have in Jesus so you can know the mind of Christ for every area of your life.

Every promise in God's Word reveals the thoughts, feelings and purposes of God's heart toward you in Christ. They actually reveal your true identity in Him. 2 Corinthians 1:20 says, *"For no matter how many promises God has made, they are "Yes" in Christ. And so through him the "Amen" is spoken by us to the glory of God"* (NIV).

Remember, as you read each promise, that you have the mind of Christ, and you hold the thoughts, feelings and purposes of His heart for your life! You can trust the Holy Spirit to manifest each one in your life.

The Mind of Christ for Your Children

Isaiah 59:20-21: *"The Redeemer will come to Jerusalem to buy back those in Israel who have turned from their sins,"* says the Lord. *"And this is my covenant with them,"* says the Lord. *"My Spirit will not leave them, and neither will these words I have given you. They will be on your lips and on the lips of your children and your children's children forever. I, the Lord, have spoken"* (NLT).

Isaiah 59:20-21 is one of my favorite promises for my children. Now that I understand what the mind of Christ is, when I read this promise, I hear the Father say, "I will manifest the mind of Christ in your children and your grandchildren's hearts and lives! For My Spirit will be in them and My Word will be spoken by them!" What a beautiful promise of God!

Isaiah 54:13: *"I will teach all your children, and they will enjoy great peace"* (NLT).

Isaiah 49:25: *"I will contend with those who contend with you, and your children I will save"* (NIV).

Psalm 112:1-2: *"Everyone who loves the Lord and delights in him will cherish his words and be blessed beyond expectation. Their descendants will be prosperous and influential. Every generation of his godly lovers will experience his favor"* (TPT).

Proverbs 11:21: *"And you can also be very sure God will rescue the children of the godly"* (TLB).

Psalm 103:17: *"Your faithfulness to keep every gracious promise you've made passes from parents, to children, to grandchildren, and beyond"* (TPT).

Psalm 103:17: *"But from everlasting to everlasting the Lord's love is with those who fear him, and his righteousness with their children's children"* (NIV).

1 Thessalonians 5:23-24: *"And may the God of peace Himself sanctify you through and through [separate you from profane things, make you pure and wholly consecrated to God]; and may your spirit and soul and body be preserved sound and complete [and found] blameless at the coming of our Lord Jesus Christ (the Messiah). Faithful is He Who is calling you [to Himself] and utterly trustworthy, and He will also do it [fulfill His call by hallowing and keeping you]"* (AMPC).

The Mind of Christ for Your Finances

2 Corinthians 9:8: *"And God is able to bless you abundantly, so that in all things at all times, having all that you need, you will abound in every good work"* (NIV).

2 Corinthians 9:11: *"You will be enriched in every way so that you can be generous on every occasion, and through us your generosity will result in thanksgiving to God"* (NIV).

Philippians 4:19: *"And my God will meet all your needs according to the riches of his glory in Christ Jesus"* (NIV).

Psalm 37:18-19: *"Day by day the Lord takes care of the innocent, and they will receive an inheritance that lasts forever. They will not be disgraced in hard times; even in famine they will have more than enough"* (NLT).

The Mind of Christ for Your Health

1 Peter 2:24: *"He personally bore our sins in His [own] body on the tree [as on an altar and offered Himself on it], that we might die (cease to exist) to sin and live to righteousness. By His wounds you have been healed"* (AMPC).

Psalm 103: 2-5: *"Let all that I am praise the Lord; may I never forget the good things he does for me. He forgives all my sins and heals all my diseases He redeems me from death and crowns me with love and tender mercies. He fills my life with good things. My youth is renewed like the eagle's!"* (NLT).

Proverbs 4:20-24: *"My child, pay attention to what I say. Listen carefully to my words. Don't lose sight of them. Let them penetrate deep into your heart, for they bring life to those who find them, and healing to their whole body"* (NLT).

The Mind of Christ When Making Decisions

Proverbs 16:3: *"Roll your works upon the Lord [commit and trust them wholly to Him; He will cause your thoughts to become agreeable to His will, and] so shall your plans be established and succeed"* (AMPC).

Proverbs 3:5-6: *"Trust in the Lord completely, and do not rely on your own opinions. With all your heart rely on him to guide you, and he will lead you in every decision you make.⁶ Become intimate with him in whatever you do, and he will lead you wherever you go"* (TPT).

The Mind of Christ for Your Marriage

Ephesians 5:25-31: *"Husbands, love your wives as Christ loved the church and gave himself for it to make it belong to God. Christ used the word to make the church clean by washing it with water. He died so that he could give the church to himself like a bride in all her beauty. He died so that the church could be pure and without fault, with no evil or sin or any other wrong thing in it. In the same way, husbands should love their wives as they love their own bodies. The man who loves his wife loves himself. No one ever hates his own body, but feeds and takes care of it. And that is what Christ does for the church, because we are parts of his body. The Scripture says, 'So a man will leave his father and mother and be united with his wife, and the two will become one body'"* (NCV).

1 Peter 3:2: *"When they observe the pure and modest way in which you conduct yourselves, together with your reverence [for your husband; you are to feel for him all that reverence includes: to respect, defer to, revere him—to honor, esteem, appreciate, prize, and, in the human sense, to adore him, that is, to admire, praise, be devoted to, deeply love, and enjoy your husband]"* (AMPC).

The Mind of Christ Concerning
God's Plan for Your Life

Jeremiah 29:11: *"For I know the plans I have for you,"* declares the Lord, *"plans to prosper you and not to harm you, plans to give you hope and a future"* (NIV).

Romans 8:28: *"So we are convinced that every detail of our lives is continually woven together to fit into God's perfect plan of bringing good into our lives, for we are his lovers who have been called to fulfill his designed purpose"* (TPT).

Hebrews 13:20-21: *"Now may the God who brought us peace by raising from the dead our Lord Jesus Christ so that he would be the Great Shepherd of his flock; and by the power of the blood of the eternal covenant may he work perfection into every part of you giving you all that you need to fulfill your destiny. And may he express through you all that is excellent and pleasing to him through your life-union with Jesus the Anointed One who is to receive all glory forever! Amen!"* (TPT).

Prayer of Salvation

Heavenly Father, I believe that Jesus Christ died to take away all my sin and rose again to make me one with Him. Today I receive Your abundance of grace toward me and Your free gift of righteousness in Christ! Today I say, "Yes!" to Jesus and I receive Him as my Lord and Savior. Thank You for the gift of eternal life. I love You because You first loved me!

John 3:16-17:

"16 For this is how much God loved the world—he gave his one and only, unique Son as a gift. So now everyone who believes in him will never perish but experience everlasting life. 17 God did not send his Son into the world to judge and condemn the world, but to be its Savior and rescue it!" (TPT).

If you prayed this prayer and believed on Jesus, you became a brand-new creation in Christ Jesus. You became the bride of Christ! The Bible says the angels of heaven are rejoicing over you (Luke 15:10). I would love to hear from you! Please contact me at www.conniewitter.com and let me know of your decision to make Jesus the Lord of your life!

Other Books
by Connie Witter

Bible Studies by Connie Witter
    Because of Jesus
    Living Loved, Living Free
    Awake to Righteousness Volume 1
    Awake to Righteousness Volume 2
    The Greatest Love Story Ever Told
    The Lord Is My Shepherd: Psalm 23

Other Books by Connie Witter
    Lies Religion Taught Me and the Truth That Set Me Free
    Let Jesus Love the Weight Off of You!
    Living Loved, Living Free
    P.S. God Loves You
    21 Days to Discover Who You Are in Jesus
    The Inside Story Teen Devotional
    The Inside Story for Girls Devotional
    Are You a Chicken Head? I Believe What Jesus Says! -
        Children's Book

You can purchase any of these resources at:

    www.BecauseofJesus.com

We would love to hear how this book impacted your life.

To Contact the author, write:
    Connie Witter
    Because of Jesus Ministries
    PO Box 3064
    Broken Arrow, OK 74013-3064
Or Email Connie at:
    Connie@conniewitter.com
For additional copies of this book go to:
    www.conniewitter.com
    or call 918-994-6500

About the Author

Connie Witter is a speaker, author, and Bible study teacher. She is the founder of Because of Jesus Ministries which was established in 2006. Her best-selling Bible study, *Because of Jesus*, was published in 2002 and is the foundation of her life and ministry.

Connie has traveled throughout the United States and internationally, sharing the life-changing message of Because of Jesus. She has been the guest speaker at churches, men and women's conferences, ladies' retreats and meetings, and has also spoken into the lives of teenagers. She has also been a guest on several Christian TV and radio programs, and has had her own nationwide weekly TV program, "Because of Jesus with Connie Witter." She also has a weekly program on her YouTube ministry channel www.youtube.com/conniewitter

Her online Bible studies can be seen worldwide through her ministry website, www.conniewitter.com, and her social media pages. Many of her Bible study series can be found on SoundCloud. Thousands of lives have been changed through her ministry. If you are interested in having Connie come speak at your event, you can contact her at:

connie@conniewitter.com

Made in the USA
Middletown, DE
20 August 2021